تَنْبِيه الإِخْوَانِ

Tanbeeh ul-Ikhwān

(Advice to the Brothers)

Regarding the Permissibility of Women
Attending the Gatherings for the Sake of
Learning the Individual Obligations (*Fard al-
'Ayn*) of the *Deen* of Allah, the Most High,
the Most Merciful

Arabic ~ English

by

Shehu

'Uthmān Dan Fodiyo

(may Allah envelop him in His Mercy – Ameen)

Translation & Commentary by
Imām Na'eem Abdullah

This book is a publication of:

Nur uz-Zamaan Institute
537 Paulson Ave
Pittsburgh, PA 15206
www.nuruzzamaaninstitute.org
store@nuruzzamaaninstitute.org

For any questions, comments, corrections, bulk purchases or to purchase a copy of this book, please contact us through our website or other contact information provided on this page.

Title:	*Tanbeeh ul-Ikhwān*
	Advice to the Brothers: Regarding the Permissibility of Women Attending the Gatherings for the Sake of Learning the Individual Obligations (*Fard al-'Ayn*) of the *Deen* of Allah, the Most High, the Most Merciful
Author:	*Shehu* 'Uthmān Dan Fodiyo
Translation:	*Imām* Na'eem Abdullah
Cover Design:	Samirah Designs Co sunnahexpressions@gmail.com
ISBN:	978-1-7340439-4-5
Publication Date:	October 3, 2021

Table of Contents

An Introduction to The Shehu

By *Imām* Na'eem Abdullah

The Shehu (pronounced "shay-who") is 'Uthman ibn Muhammad, who is better known as 'Uthman Dan Fodiyo (you will find "Fodiyo" spelled & pronounced with several variations). He was born in 1168 in the month of Safar. This corresponds with December 1754.

His younger brother Abdullahi said "He was Abu Muhammad, Uthman ibn (the son of) Muhammad ibn Uthman ibn Sālih ibn Harūn ibn Muhammad Ghurtu ibn Jubba ibn Muhammad ibn Muhammad Sanbu ibn Māsiran ibn Ayyub ibn Būba Bāba ibn Abu Bakr ibn Musa Jakolli (who arrived with our ethnic group from among the people of Toro). They are a people who originate from the lands of Futa Toro (small portion of modern-day Senegal surrounding the Senegal River), whose origin is from the Christians of Rūm or the Bani Isrā'īl. There arrived to them the armies of the *Sahābah* (Companions of the Prophet). Their ruler accepted Islam and married his daughter to `Uqba ibn Naafi`, the *mujāhid*, the Companion and the *amīr* of the West. From them was born the famous ethnicity of the *Turudbe' Fulbe'*". As for as the mother of the author, she was Hawa bint (the daughter of) Muhammad ibn Fatima bint Muhammad ibn Abdus-Samad ibn Ahmad as-Shareef ibn Ali Yanbui' ibn Abdur-Razāq ibn as-Sālih ibn al-Mubārak ibn Ahmad ibn Abul-Hassan ash-Shadhili ibn Abdullahi ibn Abdul-Jabaar ibn Tamim ibn Hurmuz ibn Hatim ibn Qusay ibn Yusef ibn Yusha` ibn

Wardi ibn Batāl ibn Ahmad ibn Muhammad ibn `Eisa ibn Muhammad ibn al-Hassan as-Sabt ibn Ali ibn Abi Tālib and Fātimah az-Zahra, the daughter of the Messenger of Allah (may Allah bless him and grant him peace and his pure Family and pleasing Companions) - Ameen. As you can see the Shehu is both Qurayshi and from among the *Ashrāf* (the Family of the Prophet) on his father's and mother's side respectively.

"Dan" is the Hausa word for son in much the same way *"ibn"* is in the Arabic Language. The meaning of *Fūdiyyu'* (or Fodiyo/Fodio) in the language of *Fulbe'* is "the jurist" (or *"faqīh"*). In other words, his father Muhammad Fuduye' was a renowned scholar.

We don't believe in what many people call reincarnation. Nevertheless, if Prophet Muhammad (may Allah bless him and grant him) were to return in the person of someone else it would have been the Shehu. The Shehu was blessed by Allah to imitate the Messenger of Allah in those areas of life where he had control of. And Allah rewarded this by blessing him to imitate the Prophet in those areas of his life where he could not possibly have had any control over – we will mention a few examples here *inshaa'Allah*.

Sultān Muhammad Bello – the *Shehu*'s illustrious biographer, successor and son (may Allah have Mercy on him) – in his book <u>Infāq ul-Maysūr</u> (Easy Expenditure Regarding the History of the Lands of Takrūr) said about his father: "The protected friends of Allah (*awliya' Allahi*) gave glad tidings of him before his appearance... An example of that is what was related by sound narrators from of Umm Hānī al-Fulānī, the righteous saintly woman who said: "There will appear in this region of the Sudan (Black Africa) a *walī* from among the protected friends of Allah (*awliya' Allah*). He will renew the *Deen* (*yujaddid ud-deen*), revive the *Sunnah* (*yuhyiy us-sunnah*) and establish the religion (*al-millah*). The fortunate people (*al-muwaffaqūn*) will follow him and his mention will be spread to distant lands (*al-fāq*). Both the common people (*al-'āmm*) and the elite (*al-khāss*) will be guided by his commands. Those connected to him will be known as the "*al-Jamaa'ah*" (the community). Among their signs is that they will not herd cattle, as is the normal custom of the Fulānī. Whoever encounters that time should follow him." In short, many of the protected friends of Allah (*awliya' Allahi*) recognized him and informed us of his affair even before his appearance and at the time of his appearance."

This is just one example of the righteous people of the past who were connected to Allah giving glad tidings of the coming of the Shehu. Prior to him, the Prophets of the past would give glad tidings of the coming of Allah's last Prophet (may Allah bless him and grant him peace). Allah makes mention of this in His Book:

(Remember) when 'Īsā, son of Maryam, said, "O children of Isrā'īl, I am a Messenger of Allah sent to you, confirming the Torah that is (sent down) before me, and giving you the good news of a Messenger who will come after me, whose name will be Ahmad." But when he came to them with manifest signs, they said, "This is a clear magic." – Qur'an: Sūrah as-Saff (61), Ayat #6.

Sultān Muhammad Bello (may Allah have Mercy on him) said: "Know, that the Shehu was groomed from his youth to be engaged in *da'wah* (inviting people) to Allah. Allah (the Most High) strengthened him by the lights of abundance. He drew him into His Divine Presence, unveiled to him the presence of his Divine Actions, Names and Attributes. He made him witness secrets of The Divine Essence. He became – by the Praises of Allah – one of the *Awliyā' Allah* (the Protected Friends of Allah); he sipped from the cups Nearness (*al-qurb*); he was adorned in the dress of Divine Realization and Love. [The Lord] of Truth (the Most High) adorned him with the crown of Divine Assistance and Guidance and equipped him for the *da'wah* to Him (the call to Allah); and a guide for the common people and the elite.

He informed me of the time when he was called by Allah, by means of the Prayer upon the Prophet (*as-Salaat 'ala n-Nabī* – may Allah bless him and grant him peace). He did the Prophet upon the Prophet without getting bored, tired or slacking. Allah assisted him with a flood illumination by means of *Shaykh* Abdul-Qādir al-Jaylī (may Allah be pleased with him) and his grandfather the Messenger [of Allah] (may Allah bless him and grant him peace). And then he witnessed the wonders of the unseen kingdoms (*al-malakūt*), the kingdom of power (*al-jabarūt*) and witnessed Divine workings of the Names, the Attributes and the Essence.

The Shehu began inviting to Allah, giving sincere advice to His servants regarding the *Deen* of Allah, destroying bad customs, destroying *Shaytān*ic innovations (*al-bid'a sh-shaytāniyyah*), reviving the *Sunnah* of Muhammad (*Sunnat ul-Muhammadiyyah*), teaching the people the individual obligations, directing them to Allah and guiding them to His obedience, removing the darkness of ignorance from them and clarifying the ambiguities for them.

He found the above-mentioned group in that [bad] condition, now counted among the successful ones who hastened to him. They were now among those who were guided and devoted to him. Then He made the people enter the *Deen* of Allah in large numbers; delegations came to him in large numbers for him; he established the Path for them to show them and made the truth clear for them."

The Shehu had his major spiritual opening at the age of 40, in the same way that the Prophet (may Allah bless him and grant him peace) was given his initial revelation at the age of 40. This is when the nickname, Nur uz-Zamaan, was given to him. He also made the *hijrah* (migration) from Degel to Gurdu in a North West direction; just like the Prophet (may Allah bless him and grant him peace) made *hijrah* from Makkah to Madinah - in a North West direction. The military battles took place after (and not before) this migration just like the Prophet (may Allah bless him and grant him peace).

He was the *Mujaddid* of his age.

عَنْ أَبِي هُرَيْرَةَ فِيمَا أَعْلَمُ عَنْ رَسُولِ اللَّهِ ﷺ قَالَ ((إِنَّ اللَّهَ يَبْعَثُ لِهَذِهِ الْأُمَّةِ عَلَى رَأْسِ كُلِّ مِائَةِ سَنَةٍ مَنْ يُجَدِّدُ لَهَا دِينَهَا))

It has come to us by way of Abu Hurayrah that the Messenger of Allah (may Allah bless him and grant him peace) has said "Verily at the head of every generation, Allah will send for this *Ummah* one who would revive the *Deen* for them."[1]

These guides or revivers – or *mujaddids* – have similar, traits, roles and responsibilities as the prophets of old. In fact, they are the inheritors of the Prophets. They have the responsibility of making things clear as they become unclear. They are the ones who uproot corruption when corruption becomes the order of the day. They are often the lone voice of truth and justice amidst a sea of falsehood and oppression. Because of the positions that these *mujaddids* take they often withstand the same trials and afflictions that the Prophets and Messengers underwent. The Prophet (may Allah bless him and grant him peace) has informed us that: "The scholars are the

---

[1] This hadith was related by Abu Dāwud Vol. #3 Hadith # 4291

inheritors of the Prophets." They not only inherit the sacred knowledge which the Prophets left behind, they also inherit the trials and afflictions of the Prophets when this knowledge is put into practice. This is one of many things that set the *mujaddid* apart from the other scholars of his time — he understands that this knowledge has a right upon him. And the right (*haqq*) that knowledge has upon the one who is blessed with it is that it be practiced and taught. Any knowledge that is gained and not practiced will be a source of grief, misery, and punishment for him in the Next Life. The noble *shaykh* Muhammad al-Maghili said in his al-Ajwiba that the *Mujaddid* will have these characteristics: "Thus it is related that at the beginning of every century Allah sends a scholar who regenerates their religion for them. There is no doubt that the state (*ahwāl*) of this scholar (*al-'ālim*) in every century in regards to [1] enjoining the right and [2] forbidding what is wrong, [3] rectifying the affairs of the people, [4] spreading justice amongst them, [5] assisting the truth against falsehood and [6] assisting the oppressed against the oppressors — be in complete contrast to the other of the scholars of his time. It is for this reason that he is like a stranger amongst them because of the uniqueness of the attributes of his state and the small number of men like him. It is then that it is made clear to all eyes that he is among the righteous and that whoever opposes and renounces him, turning people away from him, that they are among the corrupt. This is true in accordance with the words of the Prophet (may Allah bless him and grant him peace):

((بَدَأَ الْإِسْلَامُ غَرِيبًا وَ سَيَعُودُ كَمَا بَدَأَ غَرِيبًا. فَطُوبَى لِلْغُرَبَاءِ)) , قِيلَ وَ مَنِ الْغُرَبَاء يَا رَسُولَ الله ﷺ قَالَ ((الَّذِينَ يُصْلِحُونَ مَا أَفْسَدَ النَّاسُ مِنْ بَعْدِي مِنْ سُنَّتِي))

Islam began as something strange (*ghareeb*), and it would go back to the way it started – strange. So glad tidings (*tuubā*) for the strangers (*al-ghurabā'*). It was said, "Who are the strangers – O Messenger of Allah?" He said, "Those who rectify what the people have corrupted of my Sunnah."[2]

Shaykh 'Uthmān went against the grain & against the status quo just like the Prophet (may Allah bless him and grant him peace). He disturbed the unjust order of the day.

Every generation has produced revivers who have dedicated their lives to the reestablishment of al-Islam. Islam's historians and scholars have even recorded and documented who these luminaries were. And one of these luminaries was the West-African *Shaykh*, 'Uthman Dan Fodiyo.

---

[2] This hadith has been narrated on the authority of Abu Hurayrah and has been related by Muslim. The second statement regarding the description of the strangers is mentioned in the narration of *Imām* at-Tirmidhi.

The Shehu was born into a west-Africa that was at the depths of a decline which began about 300 years before his birth. The decline of Islam in Africa was kicked into high gear after the Portuguese and the Moroccans invaded the Songhay Caliphate in 1592. The primary motivations for the attack were economic. In the process, many libraries were destroyed – which contained over 50,000 Islamic and Arabic manuscripts, and over 200 scholars, including *Shaykh* Ahmadu Baba of Timbuktu, were enslaved and exiled to Morocco on March 18, 1594. With the Songhay Islamic Empire out of the way, Black Africa's protection was broken and therefore open to all of Europe to use as an endless source of slaves and other resources for the new world.

These chain of events lead to a state of major insecurity and instability in the area. Internecine warfare increased dramatically. In absence of the *Shari'ah*, paganism resurfaced which lead to the increase and prominence of the *'syncretic Muslim'* – someone who is Muslim by name; but acts, thinks, and lives his or her life exactly like a non-Muslim. Islamic scholarship was almost non-existent. 'Evil scholars' held sway over the hearts and minds of the believers who gave sanction to the various manifestations of paganism and the oppression of the rulers.

As bleak and hopeless as this situation seemed to be, it was this state of darkness which ushered in a new era of *tajdeed* – revival. There were several *mujaddid*s who emerged around the world during this period, however none of them achieved as complete of a transformation as the Shehu – Uthman Dan Fodiyo (may Allah envelop him in His Mercy) – Ameen. Upon close examination of the life of Shehu 'Uthman it becomes crystal clear that he was definitely one of the strangers described by the Messenger of Allah (may Allah bless him and grant him peace).

Our beloved Prophet Muhammad (may Allah bless him and grant him peace) was given a slave-girl by the name of Maryam as a gift. She gave birth to the Prophet's son Ibrahim who died while he was very young. Likewise, the Shehu had a right-hand possession named Maryam. She gave birth to a son named Ibrahim. And he also died very young – just like Ibrahim ibn Muhammad (may Allah bless him and grant him peace).

When the Messenger of Allah (may Allah bless him and grant him peace) was on his deathbed suffering from his final illness he was once visited by his beloved daughter Fatimah (may Allah grant her peace). He whispered something to her which made her cry and then something else which made her laugh. His wife Aisha (may Allah be pleased with her) tells the story:

أَنَّ عَائِشَةَ حَدَّثَتْهُ أَنَّ رَسُولَ اللهِ ﷺ دَعَا فَاطِمَةَ ابْنَتَهُ فَسَارَّهَا

فَبَكَتْ ثُمَّ سَارَّهَا فَضَحِكَتْ فَقَالَتْ عَائِشَةُ فَقُلْتُ لِفَاطِمَةَ مَا

هَذَا الَّذِي سَارَّكِ بِهِ رَسُولُ اللهِ ﷺ فَبَكَيْتِ ثُمَّ سَارَّكِ فَضَحِكْتِ

قَالَتْ سَارَّنِي فَأَخْبَرَنِي بِمَوْتِهِ فَبَكَيْتُ ثُمَّ سَارَّنِي فَأَخْبَرَنِي أَنِّي أَوَّلُ مَنْ يَتْبَعُهُ مِنْ أَهْلِهِ فَضَحِكْتُ

It was narrated on the authority of 'Aisha that the Messenger of Allah (may Allah bless him and grant him peace) called Fātimah – his daughter – and whispered to her, and she wept. Then he whispered to her again and she smiled. 'Aisha said: "I said to Fātimah: 'What is it that the Messenger of Allah (may Allah bless him and grant him peace) whispered to you and you wept, then he whispered to you and you smiled?' She said: 'He whispered to me and told me of his death, so I wept, then he whispered to me and told me that I would be the first one of his family to follow him, so I smiled.'"[3]

Likewise, a similar situation happened to the Shehu. Waziri Junayd (may Allah have Mercy upon him) relates "He settled there (in Sokoto) and organized the town. It became the center of Islam in this country and will remain so, if Allah wills, until the Day of Judgment. After his arrival in Sokoto, he asked his daughter Fatimah how old she was and she told him she was 28. That made her think that the time of her death had been unveiled to him but he denied it, saying instead that when she had completed 30 years of age an important event would take place. When she

---

[3] This hadith has been related by Muslim in his <u>Sahih</u>.

reached 30 the Shehu himself died (may Allah have Mercy upon him)."[4]

So, not only did both the Prophet and the Shehu have daughters named Fātimah; but they both gave them glad tidings of future events related to their own mortality!

When the Messenger of Allah was afflicted with his final illness he maintained his rotation between the houses of his wives until this became too burdensome. All of his wives gave him permission to remain in the house of his wife A'isha (may Allah be pleased with her) until Allah took his soul. The situation was the same with the Shehu. Gidadu said "In Sokoto, during the sickness in which he died (may Allah be pleased with him) he was transferred on the backs of people on his bed from house to house, until it became inconvenient to continue carrying him. Therefore, all of his wives gathered into the home of one of his wives, which was the home of our mother Hawwā' until he eventually died. It is her home in which the *Rawdah* of the *Shehu* lies (may Allah be pleased with him).

He lived to see all of his enemies either join his ranks or killed, just like the Prophet. Allah even took his soul at the age of 63 just like the Prophet (may Allah bless him and grant him peace)! Shehu 'Uthman Dan Fodiyo died at the age of 63 on Monday, 27 Jumād ul-Ākhir in 1232 A.H.

---

[4] Ibraheem Sulaiman, The African Caliphate: The Life, Works & Teaching of Shaykh Usman Dan Fodio (New York Diwan Press Ltd, 2009), 276.

which corresponds with April 21, 1817. May Allah bless the Shehu, his family, his *jamaa'ah* and continue to make him a *wasīlah* between us and the Messenger of Allah (may Allah bless him and grant him peace) until the Day of Judgment!

"...in every country that you go to, usually the degree of progress can never be separated from the woman. If you are in country that's progressive, the woman is progressive. If you are in a country that reflects the consciousness toward the importance of education, it is because the woman is aware of the importance of education. But in every backward country you'll find the women are backward, and in every country where education is not stressed it's because the women don't have education..."

– Malcolm X (may Allah have Mercy on him)

Our Sisters – The Precious Treasure of this World

By *Imām* Na'eem Abdullah

All praises are due to Allah, the Lord of the worlds. The best prayers and most abundant peace be upon our master (*sayyidina*) Muhammad and upon his Family and Companions – all of them. May Allah (the Most High) be pleased with the masters (*as-sādāti*) of the *Tābi'een*, the right-acting *'ulamā'*, and the four *Imāms* who exercised independent judgment and those who follow them until the Day of Judgment. As to what follows:

In writing this I hope to accomplish 3 things which will benefit you in this short forward – May Allah give you and I success in this – *Ameen*: [1] I hope to give you the context in which this book was written. What was going on or what happened which inspired the Shehu to write this book defending the rights of our sisters to seek a proper Islamic Education? [2] I also hope to open your eyes to the fact that nation-building – or establishing Madinah…the Muslims community/society…as we call it – is not possible unless and until the sisters are mobilized by means of education. And finally [3] I wish to encourage us to prioritize the proper education of our sisters right now!

When the Shehu was teaching – and this was before he came into open conflict with the rulers, before the *hijrah* and definitely before the *Jihād* – women would come to his lectures. You see, he was an itinerate teacher.

He would go from town to town teaching the grassroots or common people. You have to remember that most of these people were Muslim already, however, in name only. Thus, the Islamic etiquette and *adab* of those coming to his classes and lectures was less than perfect.

At the same time, the animosity of the more established scholars increased as the Shehu's popularity increased. So they would look for any way to discredit and undermine his movement and momentum.

His scholarly younger brother *Shaykh* Abdullahi Dan Fodiyo (may Allah have Mercy upon him) says that they stayed in Zamfara to invite its people to Allah. "We stayed therein for almost five years, and it was a land in which the people's ignorance was overwhelming. Most of its people had never smelt the fragrance of Islam. They would come to the Shehu's gatherings mixing with their women and he would separate them, reminding them that it is forbidden for men and women to intermingle.

He would then teach them the pillars of Islam. And then some evil people spread the rumor that the lecture was a meeting place for men and women. When we arrived at a place called Daura, an erudite scholar of Borno origin named Mustafa – known by the nickname Gwani which means expert – came to us, meeting us with his poem in which he instructed the Shehu to prevent women from coming to his lectures." These are the relevant lines from his 13 line poem:

"O Ibn Fudi! Rise to warn the people of ignorance,

That perhaps they will understand the Religion and the world.
Stop women from coming to your lectures,
The mingling of men and women is enough of a great evil.
Do not do what leads to shameful things,
Allah has not ordered the doing of any shameful thing which will harm us..."

Then the Shehu said to me 'You are the right person to respond to his lines of poetry, O Abdullahi.'" So he responded to him with his own poem. However, this did not bring an end to the debate on women's education. This book is but one of several books written by the Shehu wherein he goes against the grain prevalent during his time and safeguards the women's right to education.

The Divine Guidance or Divine Law, known as *Shari'ah* has been revealed to preserve six things. These things are commonly referred to as the 6 universals, essentials or necessities – or *kulliyāt* in Arabic. They are **[1]** *Deen* (religion), **[2]** *Nafs* (life or soul), **[3]** *'Aql* (intellect), **[4]** *Nasab* (lineage), **[5]** *Māl* (wealth) and **[6]** *'Ird* (honor & respect). The most important of the six is religion (*Deen*) because the preservation of the others is only a means of preserving it. Preservation of these 6 *kulliyāt* is an obligation and every command or prohibition legislated by Allah is meant to protect these things.

If you take into consideration everything that has been mentioned thus far you will see that the evil associated with the intermingling of men and women goes back to a breach in the preservation of *Nasab* (lineage) –

because of the fear of *zinā'* (fornication and adultery). Meanwhile the sustained ignorance of our women is in reality undermining preservation of the *Deen* (Religion). Therefore, even if there was intermingling between men and women during the Shehu's lectures, that is a lesser evil than keeping the women in ignorance of Allah's *Deen* thereby making them fuel for the Hell-Fire! And any scholar worth the label would know this!

Uthmān Dan Fodiyo's stance on women's education was uncompromising and he went completely against most of the other scholars of his time. He differed with them on many issues; however the issue of women's education was so important that he dedicated more than one book to it.

They didn't have his insight or foresight because he was the *mujaddid* of the age. And the *mujaddid* always appears when the society, especially the scholars, is completely decadent. Their shallow positions are the sickness of the society. And they are the reason why Islam and Muslims are on the decline while they think they are the gatekeepers of the Islamic tradition. The Messenger of Allah (may Allah bless him and grant him peace) said, "The destruction (*halāk*) of my community will come about because of a corrupt scholar (*'ālimun fājirun*) and an ignorant worshiper (*'ābidun jāhilun*)."

The revival of the *Deen* in any time or place is completely dependent upon education. To neglect the education of women would have defeated the *tajdeed* movement (revival movement) in two ways. As Ibraheen Sulaiman said, "Women formed not only an integral part of society, but also constituted its larger, more basic and more solid part. As the custodians of the home, which is the foundation of society, they are the most important factors in the stabilization of society. Secondly, women's role in bringing up children imbued with the spirit and orientation of the emerging order, which would need at least one generation to take root, could not be over-emphasized. The youth are the pillar of any revolution in so far as it is their energy and zeal that give it the requisite strength and vitality to challenge the prevailing order to the end. And the youth are principally formed by women."[5]

This is something that our American Muslim Martyr Malcolm X – el-Hajj Malik el-Shabazz (may Allah have Mercy on him) – understood by observations made while traveling the Muslim world. During an interview on a radio show in Paris in November 1964 he arrived at the same conclusions:

"...in every country that you go to, usually the degree of progress can never be separated from the woman. If you are in country that's progressive, the woman is progressive. If you are in a country that reflects the consciousness toward the importance of education, it is because the woman is aware of the importance of education. But in every backward country you'll find the women are backward, and in every country where

---

[5] Ibraheem Sulaiman, The African Caliphate: The Life, Works & Teaching of Shaykh Usman Dan Fodio (New York Diwan Press Ltd, 2009), 149.

education is not stressed it's because the women don't have education..."

The Shehu said "O my brothers work hard (*fa-jtahiduu*) in teaching the woman, children and the servants about the Science of *Tawheed* (*'ilm at-Tawheed*), the religious sciences and the rest of the sciences of behavior (*al-mu'āmalāt*). And whoever teaches them will be safe (*salima*) from the punishment of Allah. And if not, then he has destroyed himself, destroyed them (i.e. his family) and destined them to the hellfire (*an-Nar*)."[6]

The education of women is an Islamic obligation (i.e. it is *wājib*), therefore anyone who neglects, hinders or opposes their education is sinful and leaves himself open to Allah's punishment. This is the case for husbands, Muslim authority or leadership and even women themselves if they don't make an effort to learn enough to fulfill their obligations.

Allah (the Most High) says, "O you who believe. Save yourselves and your families from the Fire whose fuel is men and stones."[7] All of the *Mufassireen* (scholars of Qur'anic commentary), such as Abdullahi Dan Fodiyo in his *Diya' at-Ta'weel fee Ma'āni at-Tanzeel*, say that we save ourselves by abandoning Allah's prohibitions and performing His obligations. And we save our families by means of sincere advice and education, discipline, and rearing in obedience to Allah.

---

[6] *Shehu 'Uthmān Dan Fodiyo, Watheeqat ul-Ikhwān: A Message for the Brethren* (Nur uz-Zamaan Institute, 2021), 43.

[7] Qur'an: Surah at-Tahreem (66), verse 6

Islam is a complete system and way of life. Everything necessary for human salvation is found within the *Deen*. Some ill-informed people inside and outside of the Muslim Community believe there is a need for feminism or a feminist reconfiguration of Islam because of a real or perceived mistreatment of Muslim Women. This is a fallacy! The mistreatment of women in the Muslim community occurs when Islam is misinterpreted, neglected, ignored or overshadowed by pre-Islamic cultures which have the mistreatment of women embedded within them. If and when our Islamic practice improves, the mistreatment of Muslim women will simultaneously decrease. Their liberation is built into Islam itself.

In conclusion, if we are sincerely concerned about the betterment of our families, communities and the society we must prioritize the protection and education of our women! They are the key! Our Muslim women are the precious treasure of this world. They can't be oppressed, neglected or ignored. If our Muslim sisters aren't educated, mobilized and given all of the tools needed to draw closer to Allah then nothing else we do will be successful; and if we are granted some small fraction of success then it won't even last one generation because the knowledge and the ingredients for success need to be passed on to our children and no one else can do that like our sisters can!

It is my prayer that after reading this book by the *Mujaddid* of the Age – the one who made use of the methodology of the Messenger of Allah (may Allah bless him and grant him peace), made it relevant for his time and subsequently changed his society – that we see how critically important it is that we educate and mobilize our sisters in this *tajdeed* movement. Success is with Allah!

بِسْمِ اللهِ الرَّحْمَنْ الرَّحِيمِ وَ صَلَّى اللهُ عَلَى سَيِّدِنَا مُحَمَّدٍ وَ

آلِهِ وَ صَحْبِهِ وَ سَلَّمَ تَسْلِيمًا قَالَ الْعَبْدُ الْفَقِيرُ الْمُضْطَرُّ

لِرَحْمَةِ رَبِّهِ عُثْمَانُ بْنُ مُحَمَّدِ بْنِ عُثْمَانَ الْمَعْرُوفُ بِابْنِ

فُودِيَ تَغَمَّدَهُ اللهُ بِرَحْمَتِهِ آمِينَ، الْحَمْدُ لِلَّهِ رَبِّ الْعَالَمِينَ ،

أَفْضَلُ الصَّلَاةِ وَ أَتَمُّ التَّسْلِيمِ عَلَى سَيِّدِنَا مُحَمَّدٍ وَ عَلَى آلِهِ

وَ صَحْبِهِ أَجْمَعِينَ وَ رَضِيَ اللهُ تَعَالَى عَنِ السَّادَاتِ التَّابِعِينَ

وَ الْعُلَمَاءِ الْعَامِلِينَ وَ الْأَئِمَّةِ الْأَرْبَعَةِ الْمُجْتَهِدِينَ وَ مُقَلِّدِيهِمْ

إِلَى يَوْمِ الدِّينِ أَمَّا بَعْدُ

Author's Introduction

In the name of Allah, Most Gracious, Most Merciful. May Allah send peace and blessings upon our Master Muhammad, his Family and his Companions. The poor slave in need of the Mercy of his Lord: 'Uthman, the son of Muhammad, the son of 'Uthmān — better known as Dan Fodiyo (may Allah envelop him in His Mercy — Ameen) says:

All praises are due to Allah, the Lord of the worlds. The best prayers and most abundant peace be upon our master (*sayyidina*) Muhammad and upon his Family and Companions — all of them. May Allah (the Most High) be pleased with the masters (*as-sādāti*) of the *Tābi'een*, the right-acting *'ulamā'*, and the four *Imāms* who exercised independent judgment and those who follow them until the Day of Judgment. As to what follows (*amma ba'd*):

تَنْبِيهُ الْإِخْوَانِ

فَهَذَا كِتَابُ تَنْبِيهِ الْإِخْوَانِ عَلَى جَوَازِ اتِّخَاذِ الْمَجْلِسِ لِأَجْلِ تَعْلِيمِ النِّسْوَانِ عِلْمَ فُرُوضِ الْأَعْيَانِ مِنْ دِينِ اللهِ تَعَالَى الرَّحْمَنِ فَأَقُولُ وَ بِاللهِ التَّوْفِيقُ أَنَّ سَبَبَ تَأْلِيفِ هَذَا الْكِتَابِ مَا بَلَّغَنِي أَنَّ بَعْضَ الْإِخْوَانِ كَانَ يَعْتَرِضُ عَلَيَّ بِسَبَبِ حُضُورِ النِّسَاءِ فِي مَجْلِسِ وَعْظِي وَ يَقُولُ أَنَّ ذَلِكَ لَا يَجُوزُ، وَقَدْ أَفْتَى ابْنُ عَرَفَةَ بِمَنْعِ خُرُوجِهِنَّ لِمَجْلِسِ الْعِلْمِ وَ الذِّكْرِ وَ الْوَعْظِ

Tanbeeh ul-Ikhwān/Advice to the Brothers

This is the book named "Advice to the Brothers[8] – Regarding the Permissibility of Women Attending the Gatherings for the Sake of Learning the Individual Obligations (*Fard al-'Ayn*) of the *Deen* of Allah, the Most High, the Most Merciful." I say – and success is from Allah – that the reason for composing this book is that it has come to my attention that some of the brothers are opposed to me because of the presence of women in my lectures (of sacred knowledge) and they are of the opinion that this is not permissible (*laa yajūz*).

Ibn 'Arafah[9] was of the opinion that they should be prevented from going out to the gatherings of *al-'ilm* (sacred knowledge), *dhikr* (remembrance of Allah) and admonition.

---

[8] The Shehu has many books with the term "*ikhwān*" (or brothers) in the title. *Ikhwān* is the plural of "*akh*" which means "brother". The plural is used for a group consisting of all males or a group of males and females. *Ikhwān*, generally speaking, is referring to the Muslims in general; however, the Shehu is specifically referring to all of the believing Muslims who have consciously taken up the banner of social reform (*tajdeed*) along with him – particularly, the scholars and the students.

[9] He is Abu Abdullah Muhammad Ibn 'Arafah al-Warghammī, born in 716 AH/1316 CE in Tunis. He died in 803 AH/1401 CE in the same city. He was a great Tunisian *Imām* and *Mufti*; was *Ash'arī* in *'Aqeedah* (Creed;) and one of the most staunch proponents of the *Madhhāb* of *Imām* Mālik (may Allah have mercy on him).

وَ لَمْ يَطَّلِعْ أَنَّ أَحَدًا مِنَ الْعُلَمَاءِ لَمْ يَمْنَعْ خُرُوجَهُنَّ إِنْ كَانَ لِطَلَبِ فُرُوضِ الْأَعْيَانِ وَ عَدْمُ ذَلِكَ مِنْ أَزْوَاجِهِنَّ، وَ إِنَّ كَلَامَ ابْنِ عَرَفَةَ وَ غَيْرِهِ مِمَّنْ مَنَعَ خُرُوجَهُنَّ لِمَا ذُكِرَ مَخْصُوصٌ بِمَجْلِسٍ فِيهِ إِخْتِلَاطُ الرِّجَالِ وَ النِّسَاءِ بِأَنْ تَتَضَامَ أَجْسَادُهُمْ كَمَا فَسَّرَهُ ابْنُ حَجَرِ الْهَيْتَمِي فِي الْفَتْحِ الْمُبِينِ شَرْحِ الْأَرْبَعِينَ النَّوَوِيَّةِ، وَ ذَلِكَ حَرَامٌ عَلَى الْإِجْمَاعِ إِنْ كَانَ خُرُوجُهُنَّ لِمَجْلِسٍ مُطْلَقِ الْعِلْمِ، وَ أَمَّا إِنْ لَمْ يَكُنْ إِخْتِلَاطٌ بِأَنْ كَانَ ثَمَّ حِجَابٌ، وَ كَانَ خُرُوجُهُنَّ لِطَلَبِ عِلْمِ فُرُوضِ الْأَعْيَانِ فَلَا يَنْبَغِي أَنْ يَخْتَلِفَ إِثْنَانِ أَنَّ ذَلِكَ جَائِزٌ عَلَى الْإِجْمَاعِ

However, no one from among the scholars has ever prevented the women from coming out of their homes to seek knowledge of the Individual Obligations (*Fard al-'Ayn*) when they could not get this (knowledge) from their husbands.

When Ibn 'Arafah and others speak of preventing the women from coming out of their homes, they are actually referring to specific gatherings where the men and women are actually physically mixing together. And this is how Ibn Hajar al-Haytamī[10] explained it in his book <u>al-Fath ul-Mubeen Shahr il-Arba'een an-Nawawī</u> – that it is *harām* (not permissible) by *ijmā'* (consensus), if the women come out to the general gatherings of knowledge.

But as far as the gatherings where there is no mingling (of the sexes), there is a *hijāb* (barrier) in place, and they are coming out seeking to learn their *Fard al-'Ayn;* then there aren't two people who would disagree about this being *jā'iz* (permissible) by *ijmā'* (consensus).

---

[10] He is *Shihab ud-Deen* Abu ul-'Abbās Ahmad ibn Muhammad ibn 'Ali ibn Hajar al-Haytamī al-Makkī. The *Imām* was born in Abu Haytam which is in Egypt in 909 AH/1503 CE. He was Ash'arī in *'Aqeedah* and Shāfi'ī in *Fiqh* (outward practice). He was given the honorific title "*Shaykh ul-Islam*". He was a student of Zakariyyah al-Ansarī who represents the foremost resource for legal opinion (*fatwa*) in the entire later Shāfi'ī school. He died in 974 AH/1566 CE and was buried in Makkah. The *Shehu* quotes him often in many of his books.

وَقَدْ كُنْتُ أُعَلِّمُ الرِّجَالَ فُرُوضَ الْأَعْيَانِ وَ تَحْضُرُ النِّسَاءُ

مِنْ وَرَاءِ حِجَابٍ وَ أَنْهَاهُنَّ مِنْ مُخَالَطَةِ الرِّجَالِ، وَ أُكَرِّرُ

فِي الْمَجْلِسِ قَوْلِي إِنَّ إِخْتِلَاطَ الرِّجَالِ وَ النِّسَاءِ حَرَامٌ حَتَّى

صَارَ ذَلِكَ مَعْلُومًا بِالضَّرُورَةِ ثُمَّ أَفْرَدْتُ لِلرِّجَالِ يَوْمَهُمْ وَ

لِلنِّسَاءِ يَوْمَهُنَّ لِأَنَّ ذَلِكَ أَفْضَلُ وَ أَسْلَمُ وَ فِي صَحِيحِ

الْبُخَارِيِّ بَابٌ هَلْ يُجْعَلُ لِلنِّسَاءِ يَوْمٌ عَلَى حِدَّةٍ فِي الْعِلْمِ،

حَدَّثَنَا آدَمُ قَالَ حَدَّثَنَا شُعْبَةُ قَالَ حَدَّثَنَا ابْنُ صَبْهَانِي قَالَ

سَمِعْتُ أَبَا صَالِحٍ ذَكْوَانَ يُحَدِّثُ عَنْ أَبِي سَعِيدٍ الْخُدْرِيِّ وَ

قَالَ قَالَتِ النِّسَاءُ لِلنَّبِيِّ صَلَّى اللهُ عَلَيْهِ وَ سَلَّمَ غَلَبَنَا عَلَيْكَ

الرِّجَالُ فَاجْعَلْ لَنَا يَوْمًا مِنْ نَفْسِكَ فَوَعَدَ هُنَّ يَوْمًا لَقِيَهُنَّ فِيهِ

فَوَعَظَهُنَّ فِيهِ وَ أَمَرَهُنَّ وَ هَذَا الْإِفْرَادُ يَنْبَغِي هُنَا كَمَا يَنْبَغِي

فِي مَجْلِسِ الْقَضَاءِ وَ غَيْرِهِ

I used to teach the *Fard al-'Ayn* to the men and the women used to attend and they were separated by a *hijāb* (barrier). I used to prevent them from intermingling with the men. I kept emphasizing in my lectures my statement that the intermingling of men in women is *harām* (prohibited) until it reached the point that it became common knowledge (*ma'lūm bid-darūrah*). And then I designated a specific day for [teaching] the men and a different day for [teaching] women, because this is preferable and safer.

In <u>Sahīh al-Bukhārī</u> there is a chapter named, "Should a day be set aside for women in order to teach them (separately from men)?":

"Adam related to us from Shu'bah from ibn al-Asbahānī who said, I heard Abu Sālih Dhakwān relate on the authority of Abu Sa'eed al-Khudrī who said, the women said to the Prophet (may Allah bless him and grant him peace) that, "the men have out done us by taking all of your time. Please assign a special day for us to learn from you." So he set aside one day for them wherein he would instruct and command them."

This individual (male teacher) should conduct himself in the same way he would if he were in a court proceeding or other formal setting.

فِي مُخْتَصَرِ الْخَلِيلِ، وَ يَنْبَغِي أَنْ يُفَرِّدَ وَقْتًا أَوْ يَوْمًا لِلنِّسَاءِ،

وَ فِي الْجَامِعِ شَرْحِ الْمُخْتَصَرِ فِي هَذَا الْمَحَلِّ كَانَ ابْنُ غَانِمٍ

رَحِمَهُ اللهُ يَلْبَسُ الْفَرْوَةَ وَ الْخَشْنَةَ فِي يَوْمِ النِّسَاءِ وَ يُنَكِّسُ

رَأْسَهُ، وَ قَالَ عُمَرُ بْنُ عَبْدِ الْعَزِيزِ بْنِ عَبْدِ الْمَلِكِ كُنَّا نُعَلِّمُ

الرِّجَالَ وَ الصِّبْيَانَ وَ تَحْضُرُ النِّسَاءُ مِن وَرَاءِ حِجَابٍ فَقَالَ

شَيَاطِينُ الْإِنْسِ هَذَا مُنْكَرٌ فَصَيَّرُوا تَعْلِيمَهُنَّ دِينَ اللهِ مُنْكَرًا،

وَ مَا يَنْفَعُ الْمَرْأَةُ بَقَاؤُهَا فِي الدَّارِ مَعَ مَا يُوجِبُ لَهَا الدُّخُولَ

فِي النَّارِ،

In the *Mukhtasar* of Khalīl[11], the author says, "He should set aside a special time or a separate day for the [education of] the women." In al-Jāmi'i Sharh I-Mukhtasar, the author says in his commentary on this point that, "Ibn Ghānim (may Allah have Mercy upon him) used to wear an extra layer of coarse clothing and bow his head[12] on the day he would teach the women."

'Umar ibn Abdul-Azīz ibn Abdul-Malik[13] said, "We teach the grown men and the young boys and the women who are present are behind a *hijāb* (partition)."

After all of this, the *shayāteen* (devils) from among mankind said "this is evil (*munkar*)!" By taking this position, they are in fact saying that teaching the *Deen* of Allah to women is evil (*munkar*)! Her staying at home in a state of ignorance does not benefit her except that she may enter the Hell fire.

---

[11] Khalīl ibn Ishaq al-Jundī (died ca. 1365) was an Egyptian jurisprudent in Maliki Islamic law who taught in Medinah and Cairo. His Mukhtasar, known as the "*Mukhtasar* of Khalīl", is considered an epitome of Shari'ah law according to the Mālikī Madhhab, and is regarded as the most authoritative legal manual by North and West African Muslims - Taken from John Hunwick, *The Arabic Literary Tradition of Nigeria*, from Research in African Literatures Volume 28, Number 3

[12] In other words, he would lower his gaze and not look at the women while teaching them.

[13] See our Appendix at the end of the book for a biography of 'Umar ibn Abdul-Azīz.

وَ هُمْ يَرَوْنَ النِّسَاءَ فِي مُنْكَرِ الْأَعْرَاسِ مِن رَقْصٍ وَ اخْتِلَاطٍ بِرِجَالٍ وَخُرُوجِهِنَّ مُتَزَيِّنَاتٍ فِي الْعِيدِ وَ غَيْرِهِ فَلَا يَقُولُونَ شَيْئًا مَعَ أَنَّ مَنْ أَعَانَ عَلَى ذَلِكَ بِحَاجَةٍ أَوْ كَلِمَةٍ أَوْ سَكَتَ عَنِ النَّهْيِ بِلَا خِلَافٍ فَإِنَّهُ عَاصٍ، فَإِذَا رَأَوْا بَعْضَ النِّسَاءِ يَذْهَبْنَ لِتَعَلُّمِ دِينِ اللهِ وَ فَكَاكِ رِقَابِهِنَّ مِنَ النَّارِ، قَالُوا هَذَا مُنْكَرٌ إِنْتَهَى كَلَامُهُ مُلَخَّصًا وَفِي لَوَاقِعِ الْأَنْوَارِ فِي طَبَقَاتِ الْأَخْيَارِ لِعَبْدِ الْوَهَّابِ الشَّعَرَانِي الَّذِي لَخَّصَ فِيهِ طَبَقَاتِ جَمَاعَةٍ مِنَ الْأَوْلِيَاءِ الَّذِينَ يُقْتَدَى بِهِمْ فِي طَرِيقِ اللهِ عَزَّوَ جَلَّ مِنَ الصَّحَابَةِ وَ التَّابِعِينَ إِلَى آخِرِ الْقَرْنِ التَّاسِعِ وَ بَعْضِ الْعَاشِرِ

These very same criticizers, when they see women committing acts of evil during wedding ceremonies like dancing, mixing with men, and going out overly beautified for 'Eid celebrations and other events they do not say anything about these things! Those who support them in this behavior because of some need, by speech or by remaining silent about its prohibition, is indeed sinful. And there's no difference of opinion regarding that. Yet, when they see some of the women going out to learn the Deen of Allah and thereby saving themselves from the Hell-Fire they say "This is evil!""

His words are a summarized in the book called *lawāqi' il-anwār fee Tabaqāt il-Akhyār* of Abdul-Wahhāb Ash-Sha'rānī[14]. In it he summarizes the ranks of a group from among the *Awliyā*[15'] – those who are emulated in the

---

[14] He is Abul-Mawāhib Abdul-Wahhāb ibn Ahmad ibn Alī al-Ansārī al-Misrī Ash-Shāfi'ī ash-Sha'rānī and was born in 898 AH/1493 CE in Egypt. He was orphaned in his youth and relocated to Cairo where he sat with some of the greatest scholars of his time such as *Imām* as-Suyūtī. This was his situation until he became a high-ranking scholar in his own right. His most famous work is the book al-Mizān ul-Kubra (The Supreme Scale). In this text, he compares the rulings of the four schools of fiqh and categorizes their differences as either strict or lenient. He was Ash'arī in 'Aqeedah, Shāfi'ī in *fiqh* and a highly respected Sūfī. He focused a lot of his attention on the "inner branch" – meaning the affairs of the heart or *Tasawwuf* i.e. Sufism. Within the same book the Shehu is quoting in this text he exposes charlatans and impostors who claim to be from among the sufis. He recignized their evil and criticized them through revealing their ignorance, goals, and vulgarity. He died in Cairo in the year 973 AH/1565 CH.

[15] The Protected Friends of Allah – sometimes translated as "saints".

path to Allah (the Mighty and Majestic) from among the *Sahābah*[16], the *Tābi'een*[17] up until the end of the 9th century and some of the 10th century.

---

[16] The Companions of Prophet Muhammad (may Allah bless him and grant him peace). They represent the 1st generation.

[17] The Followers – those who meet the *Sahābah* and died on *Imān* (faith). They represent the 2nd generation.

قَالَ فِيهِ وَ مِنْهُمْ سَيِّدِي أَحْمَدُ بْنُ سُلَيْمَانَ الزَّاهِدُ هُوَ الشَّيْخُ الْإِمَامُ الْعَالِمُ الْعَامِلُ الرَّبَانِي شَيْخُ الطَّرِيقَةِ وَ فَقِيهُ أَهْلِهَا مُرَبِّي الرِّجَالِ فَأَحْيَا طَرِيقَ الْقَوْمِ بَعْدَ إِنْدِرَاسِهَا وَ كَانَ يُقَالُ هُوَ جُنَيْدُ الْقَوْمِ وَ كَانَ وَلِيًّا عَظِيمًا ، يَعِظُ النِّسَاءَ وَ يَحْضُرُ هُنَّ مَجْلِسًا دُونَ الرِّجَالِ يُعَلِّمُهُنَّ أَحْكَامَ دِينِهِنَّ وَ مَا عَلَيْهِنَّ مِنْ حُقُوقِ الزَّوْجِيَّةِ وَ الْجِيرَانِ،

In this book, he mentions that from among these *Awliyā' is Sayyidi* Ahmad ibn Sulayman *az-Zāhid*[18], the *shaykh*, the *Imām*, the right-acting scholar, the teaching *shaykh* of the *tareeqah* (the spiritual path), the *faqeeh* of its people and the *murabbi* of men. Thus, he revived the spiritual path of the people after it had died out. It is said that he was the "Junayd" of his people. He is a great *wali* (protected friend of Allah). He taught the women and they were present in the class without the men! They were taught the legal rulings (*ahkām*) of their *Deen* and what is obligatory upon them regarding the rights of marriage and fulfilling the rights of their neighbors.

---

[18] The abstinent one who does without worldly things.

قَالَ عَبْدُ الْوَهَّابِ الشَّعْرَانِيّ وَ عِنْدِي بِخَطِّهِ نَحْوِ سِتِّينَ كَرَاسًا فِي الْمَوَاعِظِ الَّتِي كَانَ يَعِظُهَا لَهُنَّ وَ كَانَ يَقُولُ هَؤُلَاءِ النِّسَاءِ لَا يَحْضُرْنَ دَرْسَ الْعُلَمَاءِ وَ لَا أَحَدٌ مِّنْ أَزْوَاجِهِنَّ يُعَلِّمَهُنَّ اِنْتَهَى، وَ حَكَى ذَلِكَ أَيْضًا عَبْدُ الرَّحْمَنِ فِي الْكَوَاكِبِ وَ فِي الْإِحْيَاءِ لِلْغَزَالِيّ فَإِذَا كَانَ الرَّجُلُ قَائِمًا بِتَعْلِيمِ زَوْجَتِهِ فَلَيْسَ لَهَا الْخُرُوجُ، فَإِنْ لَّمْ يَكُنْ ذَلِكَ فَلَهَا الْخُرُوجُ لِلسُّؤَالِ عَلَيْهَا ذَلِكَ، وَ يَعْصِى الرَّجُلُ بِمَنْعِهَا، وَ مَهْمَى تَعَلَّمَتْ مَا هُوَ مِنَ الْفَرَائْضِ عَلَيْهَا، فَلَيْسَ لَهَا الْخُرُوجُ إِلَى مَجْلِسِ الذِّكْرِ وَ لَا إِلَى تَعَلُّمِ فَضْلٍ إِلَّا بِرِضَاهُ اِنْتَهَى

Abdul-Wahhāb ash-Sha'rānī said: "I have in my possession about 60 of his works containing his lectures wherein he used to lecture (teach) the women. He used to say 'These are the women. They are not present in the classes of the *'ulamā'* (the scholars) nor does anyone of their husbands teach them!'"

Similar statements were also made by Abdur-Rahmān in his book <u>al-Kawākib</u>[19] and in the <u>Ihyā</u>' of [*Imām*] al-Ghazālī. Whenever there is a man present [in the home] teaching his wife it is not permissible for her to leave the home [for this purpose]. However, if this is not the case, then she must go out in order to ask questions and learn what is obligatory upon her. The husband is in a state of disobedience by preventing her [from learning]. In any case, if she is learning what is obligatory upon her, then she must not leave the home to go to the gatherings of *adh-dhikr* or to general classes unless her husband approves of it."

---

[19] This is most likely *Shaykh* Muhammad Abdur-Ra'ūf al-Munawī who wrote the book <u>al-Kawākib ad-Durriyah</u> which is an early biographical work on the Sūfī Masters. He died in the year 1031AH.

وَ قَالَ فِي الْمَدْخَلِ يَجِبُ تَعْلِيمُ الزَّوْجَةِ وَ الْأَوْلَادِ وَ الْعَبِيدِ وَ جَمِيعِ مَنْ فِي حُكْمِهِ يَلْزَمُهُ مِنْ إِيمَانٍ وَ إِحْسَانٍ وَ وُضُوءٍ وَ صَلَاةٍ وَ صَوْمٍ وَ حَيْضٍ وَ نِفَاسٍ وَ مَا يَحْتَاجُونَ مِنَ التَّصَرُّفَاتِ وَ مَا يَقَعُ مِنَ الْبِدَعِ فَإِنْ لَمْ يَكُنْ عَالِمًا تَعَلَّمَ مِنَ الْعَالِمِ الثِّقَةِ وَ يُعَلِّمُهَا كَمَا سَمِعَ، فَإِنْ لَمْ يَفْعَلْ أَذِنَ لَهَا فِي الْخُرُوجِ لِلتَّعَلُّمِ، فَإِنْ أَبَى خَرَجَتْ بِلَا إِذْنٍ وَ يَجْبُرُهُ الْحَاكِمُ عَلَى ذَلِكَ كَالنَّفَقَةِ بَلِ التَّعَلُّمُ أَعْظَمُ اِنْتَهَى ،

The author says in al-Madkhal[20] that, "It is obligatory (upon the husband) to teach his wife, his children, his servants and all of those who come under his authority. He must teach them about *Imān* (i.e. the articles of Faith, '*Aqeedah*), *Ihsān* (spirituality), purification, *Salaat* (prayer), *sawm* (fasting), *hayd* (menstruation), *nifās* (post-natal bleeding) and whatever they need for social interaction.

If the husband is not learned he should study under a reliable scholar and then teach her what he has heard. If he doesn't do that, she is permitted to leave the home for the purpose of learning. If the husband objects to her leaving the home (for the purpose of learning these things which we have just mentioned) then she must leave the home anyway – without his permission – and the ruler should force him to comply in this matter in the same way he would force the husband to pay his wife's maintenance (*an-nafaqah*). Indeed learning (Allah's *Deen*) is more important (*a'zam*) [than maintenance]!"

---

[20] This is a well known classical text quoted often by the Shehu in many of his texts. It was written by Abu Abdullah Muhammad ibn Muhammad ibn Muhammad ibn al-Hajj al-Abdarī al-Mālikī al-Fassī. He is known simply as "Ibn al-Hajj". He was 'Ash'arī in '*Aqeedah* (creed), Mālikī in *Fiqh* (outward practice) and a well known Sūfī. The full title of the text is: al-Madkhal Ash-Shar' Ash-Shareef 'Ala Al-Madhāhib which means (Introduction to Islamic Jurisprudence According to Schools of Thought). He was originally from Fez but traveled to Egypt where he died in 737AH. May Allah have Mercy on him and raise his rank.

وَ قَالَ الشَّيْخُ السَّنُسِيّ فِي شَرْحِ الْكُبْرَى فِي بَيَانِ إِهْمَالِ النَّاسِ تَعْلِيمَ الْعَآمَّةِ وَ النِّسَآءِ وَ الصِّبْيَانِ وَ الْعَبِيدِ كَأَنَّهُمْ حَيَوَانٌ بَهِيمِيٌّ لَا تَكْلِيفَ عَلَيْهِمْ،

Shaykh as-Sanusī[21] says in his <u>Sharh ul-Kubrā</u> in a discussion regarding the state of affairs wherein "the people neglect educating the common people, the women, the children and the servants - they are in fact being reduced to a state similar to that of wild animals – wherein they are not held accountable."

---

[21] He is *Imām* Abu Abdullah Muhammad ibn Yūsuf ibn 'Umar ibn Shu'ayb as-Sanūsī al-Husaynī al-Mālikī and he was born in 830 AH. He was a scholarly descendent of the Prophet (may Allah bless him and grant him peace) as his name indicates. The *Imām* was the leader of the scholars in Tilmisān which is located in modern-day Algeria. He was Mālikī in *Fiqh* (outward practice) and he wrote many books on the Islamic Belief System (*al-'Aqeedah*), among them are: <u>al-'Aqeedat ul-Kubrā</u>, <u>al-'Aqeedat us-Sughrā</u>, <u>al-'Aqeedat ul-Mukhtasira</u> and many others including the book quoted by the Shehu above which is his commentary on <u>al-'Aqeedat ul-Kubrā</u>. He was sick for 10 days before dying on Sunday the 18th of Jumād ul-Ākhīr 895 AH. After he died those around him smelled the aroma of musk. May Allah raise the rank of our *Imām*.

وَ فِي رِسَالَةِ مُحَمَّدِ بْنِ يُوسُفَ بْنِ سَالِمِ ابْنِ إِبْرَهِيمَ مِمَّا يَفْعَلُهُ كَثِيرٌ مِّنَ الْعُلَمَاءِ السُّودَانِ تَرْكُ الزَّوْجَاتِ وَ الْبَنَاتِ وَ الْعَبِيدِ مُهْمَلَةً كَالْأَنْعَامِ مِنْ غَيْرِ أَنْ يُعَلِّمُوهُمْ مَا فُرِّضَ عَلَيْهِمْ مِنْ عَقَائِدِهِمْ وَ أَحْكَامِ طَهَارَتِهِمْ وَ صِيَامِهِمْ وَ غَيْرِ ذَلِكَ مِمَّا أَوْجَبَ اللهُ عَلَيْهِمْ تَعْلِيمُهُ وَ مَا أَبَاحَ لَهُمْ مِن مَسَائِلِ بُيُوعِهِمْ وَ مَا شَاكَلَ الْبُيُوعَ وَ جَعَلُوهُمْ كَالْوِعَاءِ يَعْمَلُونَ فِيهَا حَتَّى إِذَا انْكَسَرَ يَطْرَحُونَهُ فِي الدِّمَنِ أَيْ مَوْضِعِ النَّجَاسَةِ ثُمَّ قَالَ يَا عَجَبًا كَيْفَ يَتْرُكُونَ أَزْوَاجَهُمْ وَ بَنَاتَهُمْ وَ عَبِيدَهُمْ فِي ظُلُمَاتِ الْجَهْلِ وَ هُمْ يُعَلِّمُونَ طُلَّبَاتَهُمْ صَبَاحًا وَ مَسَاءً وَ مَا ذَلِكَ إِلَّا لِأَنَّ فِي تَعْلِيمِهِمْ طُلَّبَاتِهِمْ حَظُّ أَنْفُسِهِمْ

In the Risālah of Muhammad ibn Yusuf ibn Sālim ibn Ibrahīm he says, "What most of the scholars of the Sudan (Black Africa) do is that they leave their wives, daughters and servants abandoned like animals without educating them regarding what Allah has made obligatory (*fard*) upon them in connection with their creed (*'aqeedah*), the rules connected to their purification (*tahārah*), fasting (*siyām*) and other things which Allah has made *wājib* (obligatory) upon them. Nor do they educate them regarding those things which are permissible (*mubah*) for them like buying, selling and similar things. They treat the women as if they were a pot or some container which they keep using until it breaks into pieces. And then they throw it away in the places reserved for trash and other filth (*an-najāsah*)." Then he said, "This is amazing! How can they leave their wives, daughters and servants in the darkness of ignorance while they teach their [unrelated] students day and night! This is nothing but the pursuit of their selfish ends!"[22]

---

[22] The Shehu (may Allah envelop him in His Mercy) paraphrases this same quote in his book called Nūr ul-Albāb and then he says: "This is nothing but the pursuit of their selfish ends, because they teach their students only for show (*riyaa'*) and out of pride (*fakhra*). This is a great error! Because the education of wives, children and servants is an obligation, while the education of [unrelated] students is only optional (*nafl*). And The obligation comes before (i.e. supersedes and takes precedence over) the optional – by consensus (*ijmā'*). The teaching of [unrelated] students only becomes an obligation when there is no one else to do it, and even then it is an obligation that is preceded by the obligation to educate one's family and dependents."

ثُمَّ نَادَى يَا نِسَاءَ الْمُسْلِمِينَ لَا تَسْمَعُوا أَقْوَالَ الضَّالِّينَ الْمُضِلِّينَ الَّذِينَ يَقْرَؤُونَكُنَّ وَ يَأْمُرُوكُنَّ بِطَاعَةِ الْأَزْوَاجِ مِنْ غَيْرِ أَنْ يَأْمُرُوكُنَّ بِطَاعَةِ اللهِ وَ رَسُولِهِ وَ يَقُولُونَ سَعَادَةُ الْمَرْأَةِ فِي طَاعَةِ زَوْجِهَا وَ مَا ذَلِكَ إِلَّا لِطَلَبِ غَرَضِهِمْ وَ مُرَادِهِمْ فِيكُنَّ وَ يُكَلِّفُوكُنَّ مَا لَمْ يُوجِبِ اللهُ تَعَالَى وَ لَا رَسُولِهِ عَلَيْكُنَّ مَا هُوَ كَثِيرٌ مِنْ مُرَادِهِمْ وَ لَا يُكَلِّفُوكُنَّ مَا أَوْجَبَ اللهُ وَ رَسُولُهُ عَلَيْكُنَّ مِنْ طَاعَةِ اللهِ وَ رَسُولِهِ ، نَعَمْ يَجِبُ عَلَى الزَّوْجَةِ طَاعَةُ زَوْجِهَا إِجْمَاعًا وَ لَوْ كَانَ زَوْجُهَا حَقِيرًا أَوْ عَبْدًا لَكِنْ بَعْدَ طَاعَةِ اللهِ وَ رَسُولِهِ اِنْتَهَى،

Then he addressed [the sisters directly] saying: "O Muslim women! Do not listen to the words of those who are (themselves) astray and led others astray![23] They are those who seek to deceive you by ordering you to obey your husbands without first telling you to obey Allah and His Messenger. They say that a woman's happiness lies in obedience to her husband. They say this only so that they can fulfill their own selfish ends and fulfill their selfish desires through you. They command you to do things which neither Allah (the Most High) nor His Messenger has obligated upon you. And these desires of theirs are numerous – while at the same time they do not impose upon you that which Allah and His Messenger has obligated you with. Yes, it is true that it is obligatory upon the wife – by consensus (*ijmā'a*) – to obey her husband, even if he is of low social status or even a slave. But this is only after obedience to Allah and His Messenger."

---

[23] By employing the use of the words "those who are astray (themselves) and led others astray" the *shaykh* is connecting these evil scholars who prevent, curtail or hinder the education of Muslim Women to the religious leaders foretold by the Messenger of Allah (may Allah bless him and grant him peace) mentioned in this hadith: "Verily, Allah does not take away the knowledge by taking it away from (the hearts of) the servants, but He takes it away by the death of the religious learned men (*al-'ulamā'*) until it reaches such a state where not a single religious learned man (*'ālim*) remains. The people will take the ignorant as their leaders. When these ignorant ones are questioned they will give religious verdicts without knowledge. Because of this, they are astray (themselves) and they led others astray." – This hadith has been related by *Imām* al-Bukharī on the authority of Abdullah ibn 'Amr ibn al-'Aas.

قَالَ الْغَزَالِيُّ فِي الْإِحْيَاءِ إِنَّ شَأْنَ الْفَقِيهِ وَ حِرْفَتِهِ تَبْلِيغُ مَا

بَلَغَهُ عَنْ رَسُولِ اللهِ صَلَّى اللهُ عَلَيْهِ وَ سَلَّمَ فَإِنَّ الْعُلَمَاءَ وَرِثَةُ

الْأَنْبِيَاءِ

[*Imām*] al-Ghazālī[24] said in his book <u>Ihyā' Ulūm id-Deen</u>, "Indeed, the concern of the *faqīh* [25] – and his profession – is the propagation of what has reached him from the Messenger of Allah (may Allah bless him and grant him peace) for the scholars are the inheritors of the Prophets.[26]

---

[24] Who is *Imām* al-Ghazālī? Check the Appendix in the back of this book for his brief biography.

[25] i.e. the scholar

[26] The *shaykh* is referencing the well-known hadith of the Prophet (may Allah bless him and grant him peace): A man came from Madinah to Abu Darda' while he was sitting in the masjid of Damascus. He said to him, "O Abu Dardā'! I have come to you from the City of the Prophet (may Allah bless him and grant him peace) just for a hadith which I have been informed that you narrate from the Messenger of Allah (may Allah bless him and grant him peace). And I have come for no reason other than this." Abu Dardā' then said, "Verily, I heard the Messenger of Allah (may Allah bless him and grant him peace) say, "Whoever travels a path (*tareeq*) seeking knowledge ('*ilm*) Allah will place him on a path from among the paths leading to Paradise (*al-Jannah*). Verily, the angels lower their wings for the student of knowledge (*taalib ul-'ilm*), pleased with what he is doing. The creatures in the heavens and earth seek forgiveness for the '*ālim* (*scholar*), even the fish in the water. Verily, the superiority of the scholar over the '*ābid* (devout worshipper) is like the superiority of the full moon over the other heavenly bodies. Indeed, the '*ulamā*' (scholars) are the inheritors of the Prophets. The Prophets do not leave behind wealth (literally: a *dinar* (gold coin) or a *dirham* (silver coin)) to be inherited, rather they leave '*ilm* (knowledge). Whoever takes it has taken a bountiful portion.'" This hadith has been related by *Imām* Ahmad, Abu Dāwud, at-Tirmidhī, and Ibn Mājah.

وَ كُلُّ قَادِرٍ عَلَى تَغْيِيرِ الْمُنْكَرِ فِي النَّاسِ لَا يَجُوزُ لَهُ أَنْ يُسْقُطَ ذَلِكَ عَلَى نَفْسِهِ بِالْقُعُودِ فِي الْبَيْتِ بَلْ يَلْزَمُهُ الْخُرُوجُ فَإِنْ كَانَ لَا يَقْدِرُ عَلَى تَغْيِيرِ الْبَعْضِ وَ يَحْتَرِزُ عَنْ مُشَاهَدَتِهِ وَ يَقْدِرُ عَلَى الْبَعْضِ لَزِمَهُ الْخُرُوجُ لِأَنَّ خُرُوجَهُ إِذَا كَانَ لِأَجْلِ تَغْيِيرِ مَا يَقْدِرُ عَلَيْهِ فَلَا يَضُرُّهُ مُشَاهَدَتُهُ مَا لَا يَقْدِرُ عَلَيْهِ غَرَضٌ صَحِيحٌ، فَحَقَّ عَلَى كُلِّ مُسْلِمٍ أَنْ يَبْدَأَ بِنَفْسِهِ وَ يَصُونَهَا بِالْمُوَاظَبَةِ عَلَى الْفَرَائِضِ وَ تَرْكِ الْمُحَرَّمَاتِ ثُمَّ يُعَلِّمُ ذَلِكَ أَهْلَهُ وَ أَقَارِبَهُ ثُمَّ يَتَعَدَّى بَعْدَ الْفَرَاغِ مِنْهُمْ إِلَى جِيرَانِهِ ثُمَّ أَهْلِ مَحَلَّتِهِ ثُمَّ أَهْلِ بَلَدِهِ، ثُمَّ إِلَى السَّوَادِ الْمُكْتَنِفِ لِبَلَدِهِ وَ كَذَا إِلَى أَقْصَى الْعَالَمِ فَإِنْ قَامَ بِهِ الْأَدْنَى سَقَطَ عَنِ الْأَبْعَدِ وَ إِلَّا خَرَجَ بِهِ كُلُّ قَادِرٍ عَلَيْهِ قَرِيبًا كَانَ أَوْ بَعِيدًا وَ هَذَا شُغْلُ شَاغِلٍ لِمَنْ يَهُمُّهُ أَمْرُ دِينِهِ

For everyone who has the ability to change the evil (*al-munkar*) that he witnesses being practiced among the people – it is not permissible for him to neglect his responsibility regarding [rectifying these evils] by sitting at home – only worrying about himself. On the contrary, it is incumbent upon him to go out [and rectify the evils he sees]! If he is unable to rectify some of the evil practices which he is trying to avoid, but can change another it is still incumbent upon him to go out. His going out to change what he can will not harm him if he witnesses that which he cannot change. Going out to witness a reprehensible practice without a sound reason should be avoided. It is therefore the duty of every Muslim to begin with himself and to get used to practicing the obligatory duties and avoiding forbidden practices. He should then teach that to his family and relatives. Then he must proceed to his neighbors, then to the people of his quarter, then the people of his town, then the areas surrounding his city, and so on to the furthest parts of the world. If someone who is near undertakes this duty, the responsibility is removed from those who are further away. If this doesn't happen, everyone who has the ability to [rectify these evils] must go out – regardless if he is near or far away. This is the work that preoccupies the one who cares about the affairs of his *Deen*."

انْتَهَى كَلَامُهُ وَ بِانْتِهَا بِهِ انْتَهَى كِتَابُ تَنْبِيهِ الْإِخْوَانِ عَلَى جَوَازِ اتِّخَاذِ الْمَجْلِسِ لِأَجْلِ تَعْلِيمِ النِّسْوَانِ عَلْمَ فُرُوضِ الْأَعْيَانِ مِنْ دِينِ اللهِ تَعَالَى الرَّحْمَنِ، الْحَمْدُ لِلَّهِ رَبِّ الْعَالَمِينَ، وَ أَفْضَلُ الصَّلَاةِ وَ أَتَمُّ التَّسْلِيمِ عَلَى سَيِّدِنَا مُحَمَّدٍ وَ عَلَى آلِهِ وَ صَحْبِهِ أَجْمَعِينَ وَ رَضِيَ اللهُ تَعَالَى عَنِ السَّادَاتِ التَّابِعِينَ وَ الْعُلَمَاءِ الْعَامِلِينَ وَ الْأَئِمَّةِ الْأَرْبَعَةِ الْمُجْتَهِدِينَ وَ مُقَلِّدِيهِمْ إِلَى يَوْمِ الدِّينِ اللَّهُمَّ أَرْحَمْ أُمَّةَ مُحَمَّدٍ رَحْمَةً عَامَةً آمِينَ

Here ends his words (of *Imām* al-Ghazālī) and with the ending of his words we also end this book – <u>Advice to the Brothers (*Tanbeeh ul-Ikhwān*) – Regarding the Permissibility of Women Attending the Gatherings for the Sake of Learning the Individual Obligations (*Fard al-'Ayn*) of the *Deen* of Allah, the Most High, the Most Merciful.</u>

All praises are due to Allah, the Lord of the worlds. The best prayers and most abundant peace be upon our master (*sayyidina*) Muhammad and upon his Family and Companions – all of them. May Allah (the Most High) be pleased with the masters (*as-sādāti*) of the *Tābi'een*, the right-acting *'ulamā'*, and the four *Imāms* who exercised independent judgment and those who follow them until the Day of Judgment.

O Allah! Have Mercy on the Ummah of Muhammad – an all-encompassing Mercy – Ameen!

'Umar ibn Abdul-Azīz

'Umar ibn Abdul-Azīz ibn Abdul-Malik [d. 101 A.H./720 C.E.] is the eighth ruler of the *Banī Umayyah* (the dynasty who ruled and governed the Islamic world after the Rightly-Guided Caliphs). He is from the *tābi'een* (lit. the followers) or the 2nd generation of Muslims. He is considered by many to be the 5th Rightly-Guided Khalīfah of the Muslim Ummah.

He is a direct descendant and result of the wisdom and *barakah* of 'Umar ibn-al-Khattāb, may Allah be pleased with him. It was narrated that Aslam, the freed slave of 'Umar, may Allah be pleased with him, said: "While I was with 'Umar ibn al-Khattāb as he was patrolling Madinah, he got tired and leaned against a wall in the middle of the night. He heard a woman saying to her daughter: "O' my daughter, get up and mix that milk with water." She said, "O' my mother, what about the decree of *Amir ul-Mu'mineen*?" She said, "What was his decree?" She said, "He commanded his caller to cry out: Do not dilute milk with water." She said to her, "O' my daughter, get up and dilute that milk with water, for you are in a place whether neither 'Umar nor his caller can see you." The girl said, "By Allah, I will not obey him in public and disobey him in private." 'Umar heard all of that, then he said, "O' Aslam, mark the door and remember where it is." Then he carried on with his patrol. The next day, he said, "O' Aslam, go to that place and see who said that and who she said it to, and whether they have a husband." He went to that place and found a single girl with no husband, and the other woman was her mother who had no man. He came to 'Umar and told him, and 'Umar called his sons together and said, "Does any one of you need a woman to marry? If your father had any energy none of you would beat him to this girl." 'Abdullah said, "I have a wife." 'Abdur-Rahmān said, "I have a wife." 'Asim said, "O' my father, I do not have a wife, so let me marry her." He sent for the girl and married her to Asim." She gave birth to a daughter named Layla. She later married Abdu-Aziz from (who is from Banī Umayyah) and gave birth to 'Umar ibn Abdul-Azīz, may Allah have mercy on him. The first one to write down the hadith was Ibn Shihāb Az-Zuhrī at the turn of the first century by the order of 'Umar Ibn 'Abdul 'Azīz.

He was considered by his generation to be a just ruler and a scholar. *Amir ul-Mu'mineen* 'Umar ibn Abdul 'Azīz was considered by everyone to have inherited from "*nur*" of 'Umar ibn al-Khattāb, may Allah be pleased with him. In fact, some of the elders felt as if they were reliving the blessed *khilāfah* of the first 'Umar. He returned the rights which were stolen from *Banī Hāshim* (the Prophet's clan) and other oppressed Muslims under Umayyad rule. *Imam* Ahmad ibn Hanbal went on record and declared an *ijmaa'* (Islamically binding consensus) recognizing him as the 8th Rightly-Guided *Khalifah* and the 1st *Mujaddid* foretold by the Prophet, may Allah bless him and grant him peace, in the well-known hadith - who would revive the *Deen* for the *Ummah*.

When he became the *khilāfah* it was the regular practice of the *khateeb*s (those giving the *Jumu'ah khutbah*s) to curse and abuse Alī ibn Abi Tālib, may Allah ennoble his face and be pleased with him. He abolished He prohibited any insults upon 'Ali, and his family which had become widespread within the weekly *khutbah* and instead he inserted the recitation of the Ayah: *"Verily, Allah enjoins Al-Adl and Al-Ihsân and giving (help) to kith and kin and forbids Al-Fahshâ' and Al-Munkar and Al-Baghy (i.e. All kinds of oppression), He admonishes you, that you may take heed."* [Qur'an: Sūrah an-Nahl (16); verse 90].

He was the first person to order written documentation of hadith; who did so after he was appointed to the office of *Khilāfah*. The first one to write down the hadith was Ibn Shihāb az-Zuhrī at the turn of the first century by the order of 'Umar Ibn 'Abdul 'Azīz.

'Umar Ibn 'Abdul Azīz was *Khilāfah* for only two and a half years when he was eventually poisoned in the year 101 A.H./720 C.E. by a servant who had been bribed by someone from within is own ruling family *Banī Umayyah*. His rule was short, but in that brief period he established countless good works and institutions which the world is still benefiting from! May Allah reward our *amir* – 'Umar ibn Abdul-Azīz!

Imām al-Ghazālī

He is Abū Hāmid Muhammad ibn Muhammad ibn Muhammad ibn Ahmad al-Ghazālī. The *Imām* was given the honorific title of *Hujjat ul-Islam* which means the Proof of Islam. He was born in 450 AH (1058 or 1059 CE) in Tabarān-Tūs which is about 15 miles north of modern-day Meshed, Iran.

He received his early education in his hometown and his brilliance was recognized early. He was Ash'arī in *'Aqeedah*, Shāfi'ī in *Fiqh* and is probably most well-known for being an authority in *Tasawwuf* (Islamic Spirituality also known as Sufism). The *Imām*'s studies led him to travel the Muslim world – Baghdad, Damascus, Jerusalem, Cairo, Alexandria, Makkah and Madinah. There he studied under the *Imām* of the 2 Sanctuaries until he died – al-Juwaynī (may Allah have Mercy upon him). Soon thereafter he was appointed as a teacher at the prestigious Nizāmiyya Madrasa in Baghdad.

He was undoubtedly the most influential scholar of his time and had an illustrious career when he suddenly resigned, gave up everything and went into seclusion in Damascus for 10 years. During this period he engaged in intense spiritual exercise. When he finally emerged he authored his famous seminal text named Ihyā' Ulūm id-Deen (*The Revival of the Religious Sciences*). He was and is considered to be the *Mujaddid* or *'Reviver of the Deen'* foretold by the Prophet (may Allah bless him and grant him peace) who would emerge every generation to revive the *Deen* for the *Ummah*.

He died in his hometown of Tūs in 505 AH (1111 CE). May Allah have Mercy on our *Imām*, the Proof of Islam, the Reviver of the *Deen* – *Imām* Abū Hāmid al-Ghazālī!

The Shehu – 'Uthman Dan Fodiyo (may Allah envelop him in His Mercy) – quotes from and relies heavily on the works of *Imām* al-Ghazālī. In fact, the title of his text – Ihyā' us-Sunnah wa Ihkmād ul-Bid'ah (*The Revival of the Sunnah and the Destruction of Innovation*) is an ode to the *Imām*'s Ihyā' Ulūm id-Deen (*The Revival of the Religious Sciences*). In the same way that *Imām* al-Ghazālī was declared as the *Mujaddid* after authoring that text, the Shehu was declared the *Mujaddid* of his age after writing his "Ihyā'". *Imām* al-Ghazālī's words appear most often whenever the Shehu writes on the subject of *Tasawwuf*.

Text: Maghribī Script

الله

كتاب تقبية الإخوان

على جواز اتخاذ المجلس بإقراء تعليم القرآن

علم بروق الأغيار من وزير الله تعلم الرحمن

تأليف الشيخ

مبجلا بـ بـ يدير الله أمير المؤمنين نور الزمان

عثمان بن معقد بن عثمان المغرف

با بن فودي تعقده الله برحمته

آمين

وأوأض الله علينا من بركاته وبركات علومـ

آمين

الناشر

جعفر ابن العابد العسر الكفا واصكنيو

حفظه الله ووقاه من جميع أهل الشر والسو والضر

في الشر والبشر ورزقه الله الجنة وتعينها ووالديه

وجميع المسلمين والمسلمات أميرة أمير ثم آمين

وحققوا الطبع مجمع طلع الإبار في لصعاتهـ

بسم الله الرحمن الرحيم

صلى الله على سيدنا محمد وآله وصحبه وسلم تسليما

... العبد الفقير المضطر لرحمة ربه عثمان بن محمد عثمان المعروف بابن جودى تغمده الله برحمته ... الحمد لله رب العالمين، وأفضل الصلاة وأتم ... سليم على سيدنا محمد وعلى آله وصحبه أجمعين رضوان الله تعالى عن السادات التابعين والعلماء العاملين ... ئمة الأربعة المجتهدين يرومقلدا بهم الى يوم الآبس

أما بعد

ف هـ ذا

كتاب تنبيه الإخوان

على جواز اتخاذ المجلس

لـأجر تعليم النسوان علم فروض الأعيان

مـــــن مـديـر الله تعالى الرحمن

قول وبالله التوفيق أرسبب تأليف هذا الكتاب بلغني أربعة الإخوان كان يعترض على ...بالنسب بتحضور نسا في مجلس وعظ ويقول أن ذلك لا يجوز، وقد ...نا ابن عرفة يمنع خروجهن لمجلس العلم والذكر يوعظ، ولم يطلع أراد أن العلماء لم يمنع خروجهن باركان لطلب فروض الأعيان،

Advice to the Brothers

(۲)

وعلام داكم أزواجهن، وإكلام ابن عرفة وغيره ممن
منع خروجهن لمّا ذكر خضوضهن بمجلس فيه اختلاط الرجال
والنساء، بأن تتضام أجسادهم كما أشره ابن حجر الهيتمي
في الفتح المبين شرح الأربعين النووية، وذلك حرام على الإجماع
إن كان خروجهن لمجلس مطلق العلم، وأمّا إن لم يكثر اختلاط
بأركان ثم حجاب، وكان خروجهن لطلب علم فروض الأعيان
فلا ينبغي أن يحتمله اثمار أن ذلك جائز على الإجماع،
وقد كنت لعلم الرجال فروض الأغيار وتحضر النساء
مزورا حجاب وأثّهن من مخالطة الرجال، ولا كثر
في المجلس فولح إن اختلاط الرجال والنساء حرام حتى صار
ذلك معلوما بالضرورة، ثم أفردت للرجال يوم منهم
وللنساء يوم منهن بأن ذلك أفضل وأسلم، وفي صحيح البخاري
باب هل يجعل للنساء يوم على حدة في العلم، حدثنا
آدم قال حدثنا شعبة قال حدثنا ابن صبهاني قال
سمعت أبا صالح ذكوان يحدث عن أبي سعيد الخدري
وقال قالت النساء للنبي صلى الله عليه وسلم، غلبنا عليك
الرجال فاجعل لنا يوما من نفسك فوعدهن يوم القيهن
فيه فوعظهن فيه وأمرهن وهذا الإقراء ينبغي
هناك كما ينبغي في مجلس القضاء وغيره

(٣)

وفي مختصر الخليل، وينبغي أن يبعد وقتا او يوما
سائر، وفي الجامع شرح المختصر في هذا المحل كان
غانه رحمه الله بيسر الجرءة والخشية في يوم النساء
يحضر رأسه. وفي عمر بن عبد العزيز بن عبد الملك
و بعد الرجا والصبي، ونحضر النسا مرورا صباب
ما في غير الناس هذا منكر فصيروا تعليمهن
هذا منكر ، وما ينبغ المرأة بقاواها في الدار مع
بوجب لها لا ثور في النار، وهم يرون رزور النساء
منكر الأعراس مررقص واختلاط برجال وترو بهن
ززينات في العيد وغيره فلا يقولون شيئا مع از مراعات
وذ الك بحاجة أو كلمة أو سكت عن النهى بلا خلاف وإنه
عن ، جا إذا رأوا بعض النساء يطهر لتعلم برالله وفكاك
بهر من النار، فالوا هذا منكر انتهى كلامه ملخصا
لوافع الانوار في طبقات الأخيار لعبد الوهاب الشعراني
لكن فيه طبقات جماعة من الأولياء الذير يفتدى
م بى طريبوالله عزوجل من الصحابة والتابعين الى
بالقرر التاسع و بعض العاشر، قال فيه ، ومنهم سيلا ،
مد بر بيد الزاهد هو الشيخ الإمام العالم العامل
لرباني شيخ الطريقة و بعيه اهلها مربى الرجال،

﴿ ٤ ﴾

بأساطير يوالقوم بعد اندراسها، وكان يذكر يوجدد القوم وكان وليا عظيما، يعظ النسا، ويحضرمن مجلسها دون الرجال ويعلمهن أحكام دينهن وما عليهن من حقوق الزوجية والجيران، فكان عبد الوهاب الشعراني ومن عنده، يخطه نحوستين كراسا في المواعظ التي كان يعظها لهن، وكان يقول هولا النسا، لا يحضرن درس العلماء ولا احد من أزواجهن يعلمهن انتهى، وحكى ذلك ايضا عبد الرحمن في الكواكب وفي الاحيا للغزالي فاذاكان الرجال فارها بتعليم زوجته فليس لها الخروج، فان لم يكرذالك فلها الخروج للسؤال عليهن ذلك، ويعصى الرجل بمنعها، ومهما تعلمت ماهو من فرائض عليها، فليس لها الخروج الى مجلس الـ حرولا التي تعلم فظلا الا برضاه انتهى وقال في المذخرعلى يجب تعليم الزوجة والاولاد والعبيد وجميع من في حكمه يلزمه من ايمان واغسال ووضو وصلاة، وصوم، وحيض، ونفاس وما يحتاجون من الطهريات، وما يقع من البياع، فان لم يكن عالما تعلم من العالم الثقة، ويعلمها كما سمع، فان لم يبعل اذن لها في الخروج للتعلم، فان ابى قربت بما اذر، واجبره الحاكم على ذلك كالنفقة بل التعلم اعظم انتهى، وقال الشيخ السنوسي في شرح الكبرى في بيان اهمال الناس تعليم العامة والنسا الصبيان والعبيد كانهم حيوان بهيمي

لا تكليف عليهم . وفي رسالة (٥) محمد بريوسف برسالم
بابراهيم مما يعلمه كثير من العلماء . السودان
ك الزوجات والبنات والعبيد مهملة كالانعام
غير ان يعلموهم ما افترض عليهم من عقائدهم واحكام
هارتهم وصيامهم وغير ذلك مما اوجب الله عليهم
كليمه وما ابان لهم من مسائل بيوعهم وما شاكل البيوع
يعلوهم كالوعا يعملون فيها حتى اذا انكسر بطرقونه
الماء موضع النجاسة . ثم قال يا عجبا كيف يتركون
واجهم وبناتهم وعبيدهم في ظلمات الجهل وهم
لفور طلبتهم صباحا ومساء وما ذلك الا لازي تعليمهم
لبتهم حظ انفسهم . ثم نادى يا ايها المسلمين لا تسمعوا
ولا الضلالين الفضلين الذي يريدكم ونكم ويامروكم
طاعة الازواج من غير ان يامروكم بطاعة الله ورسوله
يقولون سعادة المراة في طاعة زوجها وما ذلك الا
طلب غرضهم ومرادهم فيكم ويكلفوكم مالم يوجب الله
علي ولا رسوله عليكم ما هو كثير من مرادهم ولا يكلفوكم
اوجب الله ورسوله عليكم من طاعة الله ورسوله ، نعم
ني علي الزوجية طاعة زوجها اجماعا ولو كان زوجها
فيرا او عبدا لكن بعد طاعة الله ورسوله انتهى
كلامه ملخصا ❧ تنبيه ❧

قال الغزالي في الإحياء: إن سائر البقية وحرفته
تبليغ ما بلغه عز رسول الله صلى الله عليه وسلم وإن العلو
ورثة الأنبياء، وكل قادر على تغيير المنكر في الناس
لا يجوز له أن يسقط ذلك على نفسه بالقعود في البيت
يلزمه الخروج، فإن كان لا يقدر على تغيير البعض وعند
عرفناه عنه ويقدر على البعض لزمه الخروج لأن قدروه
إذا كان بإزاء تغيير ما يقدر عليه ولا يضره مثل هذا
مالا يقدر عليه غرض صحيح، فجب على كل مسلم أن يبدأ
بنفسه ويصونها بالمواظبة على الفرائض وترك المحرم
ثم يعلم ذلك أهله وأقاربه ثم يتعدى بعد الفراغ
منهم إلى جيرانه ثم أهل محلته ثم أهل بلده، ثم
إلى السواد المكتنفة ببلده، وكذا الوافصى العالم، فإن
قام به الأقرب سقط عن الأبعد وإلا حرج به كل قادر
فريبا كان أو بعيدا وهذا شغل شاغل لمن يهمه أمر دينه
انتهى كلامه وبانتهاء آيه انتهى كتاب تنبيه الإخوان
على جواز اتخاذ المجلس بإجازة تعليم القسم على جميع
الأعيان من يريس الله تعالى للرحمن، الحمد لله
رب العالمين وأفضل الصلاة وأتم التسليم عليه سيد بنا محمد
وعلى آله وصحبه أجمعين ورضى الله تعالى عن سادات

﴿ ٧ ﴾

التابعين والعلماء العاملين والأيمة الأربعة المجتهدين ومقلديهم اليوم اللايـن اللهم ارحم لأمة محمد رحمة عامة آمين

﴿ فايدة ﴾ وندا بزريوت الم نشر قرايا كرسورة يونكي يكرى كملو داتا تنتا صابو كنا يكر كبرا باكى ارشاء الله الله بنا كمورنمس يوئ مثننوا

فايــدة
وندا يرروير وثراءعا الله بنا كمور لمس شيطركم يربياش موغن وسواس كم بيكر نبيمسر بكرتكى شبا شاشر قرتنكى كم بياش ارزقي كوسآمً بتى يطسشبا

وقيل لماء نزراءم عليه السلام اثناء ابلير وقال إءلام اللهم اني اسالك الرب الرءوك الرحيم انت الله الرحمن الرحيم الحافظ الفقيد يا الله الحق القيوم القايم على كل نفس بما كسبت ءارينى وبر علاوه سلا

يبعث الله جبريل بقطره مسيره اربعين مرة فا وصالله الوعلام وعزنى وبلائي لايدعو يطيغ الدعاء احد مرد ربنك الهرب عنه الشيطار ود هب وسواسه عرصاءره وفرج هممومه وكشف غمومه وثاتبه النا ثياوهو راغمة وارنم يبرد هءا

فايدة   قاعتش ثيبوئ نو نور تبثى نباركا
اسامو تمنشد ومعوز ماييى انفطش آدما قوءا د ما يسرع نو نور بينا وزكيوا ان ثاء الله ، ﴿ فايدة ﴾ ان آنك شابا قام نبيبير قمى نافا طانتا بسماعتى تنتا سامس سقفر حيبقوا ارشاء الله والكاتب جعفرابن الحاج حسى الكـ وكتنو

ت كغشبى غذو وزكيوا ارشاء الله

10 Point Madinah Program

Nur uz-Zamaan Institute is committed to implementing the following points. In essence it is our intention to establish Islam. We realize that to say it is "our goal to establish Islam" is very broad and vague to many of us. Thus, the goal and mission is alluded to in the title – Madinah. We intend to establish a Madinah, a city, built upon the methodology of Prophet Muhammad, may Allah bless him and grant him peace. We also hope to work together with other communities who have the same goals. This is in obedience to Allah's words "Help ye one another in righteousness and piety" (Sūrah 5:2). The ten points mentioned in this program are well-known to be part of Islam, for the most part. However, these points or aspects of these points have been neglected, forgotten or corrupted. This program must be seen as a *Tajdeed* or a revival. The Messenger of Allah (may Allah bless him and grant him peace) said, "The Mercy of Allah is with my *Khalifah*s (successors)." It was said, "Who are your *Khalifah*s (successors)?" He said, "Those who bring my *Sunnah* to life and teach it to the people. Whoever brings my *Sunnah* back to life, has given life to me. Whoever gives life to me, will be with me in paradise." Thus we hope by embarking upon this path that we are granted companionship with Allah's beloved – may Allah bless him and grant him peace.

[1] *Aqeedah* (Proper Belief)

We intend to revive the obligation of learning and teaching what is proper regarding the belief of the Muslims (*ahlus-Sunnah wal-Jamaa'ah*). We agree that this belief must be consistently taught and internalized; and deviation from it must be strongly refuted. The belief of the Muslims is contained within books like the "Usuul ud-deen" of Shehu Uthman Dan Fodiyo, the *'Aqeedah* of *Imam* at-Tahāwiy and countless others.

[2] *Arkaan ul-Khamsa* (Five Pillars of Islam)

(a) We intend to revive the obligation of establishing the outward actions of Islam, first and foremost, the five (5) Pillars of Islam like the establishment of *Salah* (prayer) – this means that we establish a place of worship (*Jami masjid, masjid, zawiya, ribat*, etc...) and uphold the 5 congregational prayers in them. The emphasis on establishing a place of worship may not be immediately relevant for some who have already established this; but for most of us who have dedicated their lives to establishing what is outlined in these ten points, we have no *masjid* or place of worship where these principles are a priority. Therefore, it is imperative that masajid be established where these points be given their proper importance.

(b) We intend to revive, with Allah's permission, the establishment of the 3rd Pillar of Islam which is Zakāt. Our beloved Prophet, may Allah bless him and grant him peace, has taught us that "Islam is built on five (pillars):

Testifying that there is no god but Allah and that Muhammad *peace be upon him* is the Messenger of Allah, establishing the prayers, paying the Zakat, making the pilgrimage to Mecca, and fasting in Ramadan." These are known as the "Pillars of al-Islam." These pillars are the support and foundation of our way of life. If any one of these pillars/supports is weakened the entire structure is in danger of collapse. Zakat has now become known as the "forgotten Pillar" of Islam. The establishment of Zakat will ensure that the wealth of the *Jamaa'ah* (community) circulates among all of its members. Those who have the *nisaab* – which is the minimum amount of wealth requiring its owner to pay Zakat – are duty-bound to give a small percentage of their excess wealth to the leadership or his designee so that it is redistributed to the poor. Zakat, in and of itself, will take the burden off of those organizations which provide services to the poor and disenfranchised segments of our community like the homeless. We agree that Zakat and its integrals must be revived!

(c) We intend to revive the *Sunnah* of the fast of Ramadan; which must be learned, practiced and revived. Many of the Muslims do fast during this blessed month, however, because of the introduction of many modern, blameworthy innovations, the fast has become deficient. The major innovation which has infected many of our communities is the acceptance and reliance upon astronomical calculations along with the blind acceptance of the pronouncements of the ruling monarchy which is currently occupying the Arabian Peninsula (the Saudi Family). Thus we agree that it is imperative that we return to the Prophetic methodology of having a group from each *Jamaa'ah* in every locale go out every month and sight the moon; thereby developing their own local lunar calendar. It is this local sighting/calendar that the fast of Ramadan will begin and end. This will also apply to 'Eid ul-Adha as well as 'Eid ul-Fitr and the remaining months of the Lunar calendar. We agree that this must be learned and implemented.

[3] *Taalib ul-'Ilm* (Seeking Knowledge)
We intend to revive traditional methods of seeking knowledge. We agree that knowledge is gained continuously and knowledge sought is to be implemented immediately. The Prophet Muhammad, may Allah bless him and grant him peace, said "Seeking knowledge is obligatory upon every Muslim." Every point that we have mentioned thus far, and every point that we will mention, by the permission of Allah, is an action which must be preceded by knowledge. Every action that is obligatory upon us to perform is likewise accompanied by the knowledge of how to properly perform that act. For example, we know that it is mandatory for the Muslim to pray and naturally it is also obligatory upon him or her to learn how to pray. Shehu 'Uthman ibn Fudi, may Allah envelop him in His mercy said, "The obligations which are incumbent upon you from the science of **tawheed** is to know as much as is necessary to help you understand the foundations of the *Deen* (**usūl ud-deen**).... *The obligations*

which are required for you to perform are thus incumbent upon you to know. This is in order that you may accomplish them properly. These obligations include purification (*tahāra*), fasting (*sawm*), and prayer (*salāt*). As for as pilgrimage (*hajj*), (*zakāt*), and struggle (*jihād*) are concerned - these sciences are only incumbent upon you to know at the time they become obligatory for you to perform. Again, this is in order to accomplish them properly. *However, when they are not obligatory upon you to perform, then knowing them is also not obligatory...* The knowledge which is obligatory upon you to know from the science of secrets are those knowledge's which are obligatory (*wajib*) upon the heart and those which are forbidden (*nuhiya*) for it - in order to acquire esteem for Allah, sincerity, sound intention, and the soundness of action."

Along with what was mentioned we must also revive the understanding of what a scholar is. Shehu Uthman also said: "Whoever has learned a single issue (*mas'alah waahidah*) is one of the learned ones in it (*ahl l-'ilm biha*). Thus it is obligatory upon him to teach it to others, if it is one of the individually obligatory duties. Otherwise, he will have a share in the sin." With this in mind we will revive the Prophetic Sunnah of disseminating beneficial knowledge as we acquire it; Contrary to the Christian/Jewish method of creating an elite group of scholars who monopolize the divine knowledge. Because we are living in an era where the majority of us believe we must imitate the dominant culture in order to be successful, our current group of scholars/leaders are in the process of creating a modern-day "Islamic priesthood", which we categorically reject. This is in accordance with the Prophetic command: "Relate from me, even if it is a single verse (*ayah*)." Thus it should be clear that everyone has a part to play in this revival. We should all be students and teachers at the same time.

[4] *Shuurah* (Mutual Consultation)

We intend to revive the idea of conducting all of our affairs by means of mutual consultation (*shuurah*). One of the destructive qualities of our people is that once we achieve some type of leadership and/or autonomy we become over opinionated. The Prophet Muhammad, may Allah bless him and grant him peace, was receiving revelation from Allah, the Most high, but yet as he said, he had two advisors from the heavens (Angels *Jibreel* and Meekaal) and two from the earth (Abu Bakr and 'Umar). Furthermore, Allah says in the Qur'an, to "seek consultation with them in the affair" (Sūrah 3:159). In our efforts to establish Islam we realize that not one person has all of the answers, therefore, we agree to come together in order to benefit from everyone's input.

[5] *Jamaa'ah* (Community)

We intend to revive the obligation of forming and adhering to the *Jamaa'ah* (community). It is not permissible for any person or group among the Muslims to remain isolated - by themselves. For verily Allah, the Most High says, "Hold firmly to the rope of Allah all together and do not become divided" (Sūrah 3:103). Our people are afflicted with the disease of radical individualism. We are individuals, yes, but just like organs of a human body we only function properly when we come together as a whole. This is also an obligatory *Sunnah* that has been abandoned. This point and the next one are of critical importance; the reason being is that for the most part they don't exist at the moment. Umar Ibn Khattaab, may Allah be pleased with him, said "there is no Islam without a (*jamaa'ah*) community and there is no community without leadership (*imaarah*) and there is no leadership without obedience (*taa'ah*)." Therefore, the very existence of our Islam depends upon us coming together under our respective leaders, and the *seerah* confirms this.

[6] *Imaarah* (Leadership)

We agree to choose an *amir* (leader) from among ourselves. Everybody needs a head. Every tribe needs a chief. Employees need a manager. Likewise, a *Jamaa'ah* needs an *amir*. Allah says in the Qur'an "O you who believe! Obey Allah and obey His Messenger and those charged with authority (*amri*) from among you (*minkum*). " (Sūrah 4:59) Any time the Muslims come together for any purpose regardless of how mundane that purpose is, they must appoint a leader from among themselves. Allah's Prophet, may Allah bless him and grant him peace, ordered us to appoint a leader from among ourselves, even if we are traveling together on a journey. A close study of the life of the Prophet will illustrate the fact that the Muslims - whether they were away from the Prophet or close to him - always have a leader that was in charge of their affairs.

[7] *Hijrah* (Migration)

We agree to revive the Prophetic tradition of migrating for the sake of Allah. Allah says "Surely those whom the angels cause to die, while they are wronging themselves, [to them] the angels will say, 'In what circumstances were you?' They will say, 'We were weak upon the earth.'[The angels will] say, "But was not Allah's earth wide, so that you might have emigrated in it?' As for such, their refuge shall be hell" (Sūrah 4:97). There are many levels of immigration. There is the level of emigrating from what Allah has made prohibited; this is based upon the statement of the Prophet Muhammad, may Allah bless him and grant him peace, "The immigrant is he who migrates from what Allah has prohibited." The companions of the Messenger of Allah migrated to Ethiopia to preserve their Islam. They also migrated to Medina to establish Islam. This understanding of migration has to be taught and revived in the lives and hearts of the believers. On one level we must make immigration from all methodologies and foreign influences which do not have the best interests of that African-American Muslim at heart. We will no longer champion the causes of other Muslims to the detriment of our causes and interests. We categorically reject any methodology which has embedded within it a disdain for Africans in general and African Americans in particular. We do not apologize for this. We understand that many will call us nationalists but we do not care. We know from what the Messenger of Allah, may Allah bless him and grant him peace, has taught us that this is not nationalism in fact it is Islam in practice - in its purest form. We also realize that we must migrate on a physical level. We have to establish places of worship as we described above and then we have to move near those places of worship and establish our communities upon that foundation. Moving near our place of worship means that we must own the property in which we live. We know from our experience of establishing Islam in this country that when the Muslims open a masjid and clean up the area the non-Muslims buy up the property, the value of all of the property in the area increases and the Muslims who are responsible for the reinvigorated neighborhood can no longer afford to live there. With that we understand that this migration takes planning. Each community has to analyze the earning potential of its members and then pinpoint an area in which its members can afford to purchase property. We must be able to visualize this! In the same way that every major city in the United States has areas like "Chinatown" and "Little Italy", we have to have a *"Muslimtown"* or a "Madinah" which supports the culture and tradition of Islam in all of its personal and communal aspects. This *"Muslimtown"* can be one square block or it can be a whole neighborhood or city. There is no minimum requirement as far as its size. The "Madinah" of the Prophet, may Allah bless him and grant him peace was very small by today's standards.

[8] *Tasawwuf* (Spiritual Exercise/Character Reformation)

We agree to revive the science of tasawwuf, which is a part of Islam and not an addition to it. This is based upon the well-known *hadith* of the Prophet when he was questioned by angel Gabriel. One of the things that the Angel asked him was "What's *Ihsān?*" This was explained by all of our scholars like Shehu Uthman Dan Fodiyo: "I say, and success is with Allah, and may you and I be among the successful; realize that the *Deen* which Muhammad may Allah bless him and grant him peace came with has its foundations (*usūl*) and its branches (*furu`u*). As for its foundations, it is **al-imaan** and the science that verifies *al-imaan* is the foundation of the *deen* (*usuul l-deen*). As for its branches, it is divided into two: an outward branch and an inward branch. As for its outward branch, it is **al-islaam** and the science that verifies *al-islaam* is the science of the law (`ilm 'l-shari`ah). As for the inward branch, it is **al-ihsān** and the science that verifies *al-ihsaan* is the science of the reality (`ilm 'l-haqiqah)." There have been many noble attempts by communities who have preceded us to establish Islam among our people; however many of them lacked a viable spiritual component and some others were only concern with spirituality. It is as *Imām* Mālik said, "Whoever practices spiritual purification (*tasawwufa*) but does not seek understanding of the *Deen* (*tafaqqahu*) has become a heretic (*tazandaqa*). Whoever seeks understanding of the *deen* (*tafaqqahu*) but does not practice spiritual purification (*tasawwufa*) has become corrupt (*tafasaqa*). Whoever gathers the two has attained spiritual realization (*tahaqqaqu*)." To leave off spirituality is to leave off a part of Islam. Just like everything else in this beautiful way of life, there are methods which have been laid down to help us bring about this internal change.

[9] *As-Suq* (Market Place)

We intend to revive and reestablish our own marketplace. When Prophet Muhammad, may Allah bless him and grant him peace, established the city Medina – which is the model city - after building the *masjid*, the next thing he did was establish a marketplace in the middle of Medina. At that time there were other marketplaces on the outskirts of Medina which for the most part were being controlled by the future enemies of Islam and Muslims. Therefore, the Muslims must become entrepreneurial in their thinking, moving out of the employee state of mind and migrating into the employer of state of mind. In other words we have to create jobs, trades and other ways of employing our own. In order for Allah to bless our efforts, our trading practices must be sanctioned by Islamic law; which means that we have to move away from *riba'* and all of the other deceptive trading practices. This also means that we must gradually move away from the use of paper money. We must begin bartering and trading using instruments which have intrinsic value like gold and silver, i.e. the *dinar* and the *dirham*.

[10] *Hifz ul-Nasab wa l-ahl* (Preservation of Lineage and Family)

We intend to revive the importance of the family and its preservation. We agree that we must protect our family. This is not a boys club. Our families, meaning women and children, must also be involved in everything that we've mentioned thus far. If this is not the case then our efforts will die out as soon as we die. This also indicates that we must marry those who uphold the same principles that we do. This means that our families must intermarry. We must take our environment into consideration and realize that our people are inundated with sexual stimulation from every angle. With this in mind we must equip our children to marry each other even at a young age in order to prevent the destruction of our lineage by means of fornication and adultery.

The unveiling of these ten points: (1) *Aqeedah* (Proper Belief), (2) *Arkaan ul-Khamsa* (Five Pillars of Islam), (3)*Taalib ul 'ilm* (Seeking Knowledge), (4) *Shuurah* (Mutual Consultation), (5) *Jamaa'ah* (Community), (6) *Imaarah* (Leadership), (7) *Hijrah* (Migration), (8) *Tasawwuf* (Spiritual Exercise/Character Reformation), (9) *As Suq* (Marketplace), (10) *Hifz ul-Nasab wa l-ahl* (Preservation of Lineage or Family) are important steps to achieve success in practicing what our beloved Prophet Muhammad, may Allah bless him and grant him peace, brought to us by the mercy of Allah the Most High. Through this venture, *Inshaa Allah*, sweet, nutritious fruit of righteous progeny will be produced, adding the color of hope to this bleak canvas called the *dunya*. Our future generation of Muslims would continually keep these ten points embedded in their hearts and implemented on their limbs. While all the time, keeping the *nur* (light) of Islam ever shining, leading the way down the *sirat ul-mustaqeem* (the straight path)

Inshaa Allah. We welcome all those with like minds to get on board to make these ten points not a slogan, but a reality. Our desire to establish Madinah on the model of the Prophet, may Allah bless him and grant him peace, has motivated us to revive these points. We have enumerated ten (10) of them, which is consistent with the number of years that the Messenger of Allah, may Allah bless him and grant him peace, developed the first community - the 1st Madinah. And Success is with Allah.